POWER
Prayers
for Teachers

DENISE SHUMWAY

BARBOUR
PUBLISHING

© 2008 by Barbour Publishing, Inc.

ISBN 978-1-60260-192-5

All rights reserved. No part of this publication may be reproduced or transmitted for commercial purposes, except for brief quotations in printed reviews, without written permission of the publisher.

Churches and other noncommercial interests may reproduce portions of this book without the express written permission of Barbour Publishing, provided that the text does not exceed 500 words and that the text is not material quoted from another publisher. When reproducing text from this book, include the following credit line: "From *Power Prayers for Teachers,* published by Barbour Publishing, Inc. Used by permission."

Scripture quotations marked NIV are taken from the HOLY BIBLE, NEW INTERNATIONAL VERSION®. NIV®. Copyright © 1973, 1978, 1984 by International Bible Society. Used by permission of Zondervan. All rights reserved.

Scripture quotations marked NASB are taken from the New American Standard Bible, © 1960, 1962, 1963, 1968, 1971, 1972, 1973, 1975, 1977, 1995 by The Lockman Foundation. Used by permission.

Scripture quotations marked KJV are taken from the King James Version of the Bible.

Scripture quotations marked NKJV are taken from the New King James Version®. Copyright © 1982 by Thomas Nelson, Inc. Used by permission. All rights reserved.

Cover Photograph: Jeff Zaruba/Stone/Getty Images

Published by Barbour Publishing, Inc., P.O. Box 719, Uhrichsville, Ohio 44683, www.barbourbooks.com

Our mission is to publish and distribute inspirational products offering exceptional value and biblical encouragement to the masses.

 Member of the
Evangelical Christian
Publishers Association

Printed in the United States of America.

To my sister, Beve,
who has always believed in me as a writer—and
so much more. Through the years she has taught me,
not in words but by her example, because she lives a
life of prayer. I am able to write about prayer largely
because of her help and her consistent example. This
book is just one of many answers to her prayers.

Contents

Introduction

Imagine a room full of students begging to be taught your most carefully prepared lesson. You are about to instruct them on a subject near and dear to your heart, perhaps one you have devoted your life to learning. You sense the perfect intersection of your passion and your students' interest.

Impossible, you say? That's just the scene in Luke 11. Jesus finds Himself amid an eager class—His disciples—one of whom makes the request, "Lord, teach us to pray, just as John taught his disciples" (Luke 11:1 NIV). What follows is Jesus' teaching on prayer, what many call the Lord's Prayer, a few dozen words which give us a pattern for our prayer life today. Like the disciples, we can learn how to pray from our Master.

And how we need to pray! In our jobs as teachers, we face many challenges. We hold responsibility for the educational development of our classes. We want to model moral and spiritual values for our students. We're often caught in the middle of funding problems, power struggles, family breakdowns, and other negative cultural influences. And, of course, we have our own lives outside of school—our own joys and trials, our own families and friends, our own health, finances, and churches to deal with.

That's what *Power Prayers for Teachers* is all about. This book provides encouragement for you—as a teacher—to pray for your students, your school, your fellow educators, and your administrators. This book urges you to pray for yourself, seeking God's presence and His guidance to make you a better teacher, friend, family member, and Christian. This book offers biblical reasons to pray, and specific "prayer starters" to help you on your way.

Prayer was vital to Jesus. It was the source of His relationship to His Father. He lived to do the will of His Father who had sent Him (John 6:38). Doing the Father's will was his food—that which sustained Him (John 4:34). Many times in the gospels we see that Jesus went off by Himself to pray. He even prayed for us (John 17:20), those who would believe in Him through the disciples' message, that we would experience the same oneness with the Father that He does.

Let's learn together, from the greatest teacher, how to be praying teachers.

In my effort to more effectively pray as a teacher, I considered my life and divided it into the 21 headings that make up the 21 chapters of this book. I began with the foundation of my life, my relationship with God, and moved from there through my professional world then to my personal life. Finally I considered my future. In each area, I looked into the Bible to find verses that matched both the needs I saw and the means to meet them. I found myself praying for wisdom to understand Jesus as a teacher and myself as both a teacher and a learner.

I hope you'll find the same inspiration as you read through this book and that the prayers included in each chapter will launch you into your own conversations with God. As teachers, we and our students benefit when we pray!

The Power of Light

*P*salm 119:105 is a wonderful metaphor: "Your word is a lamp to my feet and a light for my path" (NIV). Of course, our Bible doesn't literally shine like headlights on a dark, winding road, but spiritually speaking, it does lead and direct us on a daily, even moment-by-moment basis down the path of life.

In ancient times, foot lamps provided just enough light for the next step. Isn't that a comforting picture? We don't need to see the path of our entire journey, only where to put our foot next. Each September as we face a new class, we don't have to be anxious about the whole school year. We just need to trust the Lord for light for the first step.

The light for our path comes from God's Word. In her book *Let Prayer Change Your Life*, author Becky Tirabassi tells when God spoke through His Word at a difficult time. Ready to speak at a high school assembly, she learned the principal doubted that she could handle the crowd—because she was a woman. Seeking confirmation of God's call on her life and assurance that He would be with her, she turned to Psalm 119 and read, "[You] will not be put to shame" (Psalm 119:46 NIV).

"Daily Bible reading, along with prayer," Tirabassi says, "encourages a two-way conversation with God." She asked, and He answered.

We need that divine guidance on a regular basis, even several times a day. While we can't leave our classes to run to our "prayer closet" each time we find ourselves in a difficult situation, we can offer silent cries for help throughout the day. God will faithfully bring to mind the Word we have stored in our hearts.

As we immerse ourselves in God's Word, it becomes a lighthouse to us, shining in the darkness and lighting our journey home. Then we can share the light with those around us.

Nineteenth-century evangelist D. L. Moody liked to tell the story of a ship that was lost on the rocks during a storm near Cleveland, Ohio. The pilot lost his way because the "lower lights" he depended on had gone out. "Brethren," Moody said, "the Master will take care of the great lighthouse; let us keep the lower lights burning." Musician Philip P. Bliss put Moody's idea into a song with the chorus,

> *Let the lower lights be burning!*
> *Send a gleam across the waves!*
> *Some poor fainting, struggling seaman*
> *You may rescue, you may save.*

Let us come to Jesus, the Light of the world, each day in the Word. His light will help us to pray more effectively. And then we can reflect His light to those in our classrooms who need help and guidance for their journeys.

Jesus — the Light of the World

"I am the light of the world. Whoever follows me will never walk in darkness, but will have the light of life."

JOHN 8:12 NIV

*L*ord Jesus, I appreciate how You guide us by Your living light, which shines through Your Word. Thank You for bringing us out of the darkness of this world. Please help me follow You more closely, so those lives I touch throughout the day will be able to see You for themselves and to experience You as the light of their lives.

The Word, a Lamp and a Light

Your word is a lamp to my feet and a light for my path.

PSALM 119:105 NIV

*S*hine today, Lord, through Your Word. Please lead me, so I can, in turn, lead in my classroom. Let me guide these precious lives toward You. Light my way for the steps I take today, and help me trust You for tomorrow's journey. I thank You for Your faithful direction in my teaching. You've been with me every step of the way.

The Great Light
The people who walk in darkness will see a great light;
those who live in a dark land, the light will shine on them.
ISAIAH 9:2 NASB

*T*hank You, Father, for Jesus, who fulfills this prophecy. He came as the great light, and He shines today through the Word and through those who follow Him. May Your light shine on those in my school who "live in a dark land." I pray that many of them will find You as the light shining through their darkness.

Believers—Lights in the World
Do all things without grumbling or disputing; so that you will
prove yourselves to be blameless and innocent, children of God
above reproach in the midst of a crooked and perverse generation,
among whom you appear as lights in the world.
PHILIPPIANS 2:14–15 NASB

*F*ather, we can't live this kind of life on our own. But as Your children, with Your life in us, we are blameless and above reproach. May we always reflect the light of Your Son and bring glory to Your name as we shine forth in our classrooms, our schools, and our communities.

Invincible Light

*In Him was life, and the life was the light of men. And the light
shines in the darkness, and the darkness did not comprehend it.*

JOHN 1:4–5 NKJV

*L*ord, You shine like a lighthouse in this black world.
There is no darkness strong enough to overtake Your
brightness. Your Word provides light for me to follow
and shines through me as life. Please open doors for me
to share this amazing reality in my school, where You
have placed me to share Your light and life.

His Radiant Commands

*The precepts of the LORD are right, giving joy to the heart. The
commands of the LORD are radiant, giving light to the eyes.*

PSALM 19:8 NIV

*F*ather, Your commands enlighten us, giving us direction
and wisdom. Your Word brings light, not darkness. Your
precepts offer joy, not condemnation. As I come to You
in Your Word, You shine in my heart, clearly indicating
the way I should go. This is a treasure beyond compare.

Bringing Glory to the Father

"Let your light shine before men in such a way that they may see your good works, and glorify your Father who is in heaven."

MATTHEW 5:16 NASB

*D*ear Father, may I always be aware that others are watching me, looking for evidence of Your presence in my life. As Your Word guides and strengthens me, may the good works You lead me to do be a powerful testimony to my coworkers and students. In this, You will be glorified, and others will know that You live in me.

God Shining in Our Hearts

For God, who said, "Let light shine out of darkness," made his light shine in our hearts to give us the light of the knowledge of the glory of God in the face of Christ.

2 CORINTHIANS 4:6 NIV

*L*ord, what a mystery! You shine within me, revealing Yourself. When You speak, physical things come into being. When You shine, lives change. I thank You for shining in me, for changing me. Shine through me today, Lord, bringing others to the glorious knowledge of who You are.

Everlasting Light

*No longer will you have the sun for light by day, nor for brightness
will the moon give you light; but you will have the LORD for an
everlasting light, and your God for your glory.*
ISAIAH 60:19 NASB

*L*ord Jesus, one day, light as we know it will change.
You will be the only light we need. And what a light
You are—glorious and everlasting! You will never
stop illuminating Your people, Father. I can trust
You to light each day of my life, both on this earth
and in the world to come.

Light and Understanding from the Word

The unfolding of your words gives light; it gives
understanding to the simple.

PSALM 119:130 NIV

*D*ear Father, I thank You for the light that shines through Your Word to my open heart. You unfold Your design to me—you enable me to understand who You are and how much I need You. Keep me simple and focused on You, always trusting You to give me the understanding I need to work with my students. Let me sense their hearts and know their true needs because of the enlightenment You provide.

Light to Believe

"I have come as Light into the world, so that everyone who believes in Me
will not remain in darkness."

JOHN 12:46 NASB

*L*ord Jesus, You came as light to give us a way out of the darkness of this world. Thank You for a way out of this sin-blinded world. Shine through me that others may see Your light and believe—and find a way out of their darkness. So many are trapped, Father, lost in the dark. May they believe today as they see You in me.

Light and Salvation

The LORD is my light and my salvation; whom shall I fear?
the LORD is the strength of my life; of whom shall I be afraid?
PSALM 27:1 KJV

*F*ather, I am so secure with You as my light, my salvation, and my strength. What rest and assurance that brings to my busy life! Remind me, when I'm tempted to be afraid, that You will never leave me in darkness. You will never leave me alone. As my strength, Lord, I can trust in You. You are my light and my salvation!

Children of Light

For you were formerly darkness, but now you are
Light in the Lord; walk as children of Light.
EPHESIANS 5:8 NASB

*D*ear Lord, I thank You for making me Your child—a child of the light. I thank You for ending the darkness of my life and filling me with Yourself, making my life a lamp that shines before others. Please, Lord, shine out as a beacon in the darkness of my school and my community, so others can know You. May many more join this family of light.

Light in Darkness

Do not gloat over me, my enemy! Though I have fallen, I will rise.
Though I sit in darkness, the LORD will be my light.
MICAH 7:8 NIV

*D*ear Lord, sometimes my way is dark. It seems that there is no light at all. But even then, You *are* light. Your Word says it, and I believe it. May that be my true experience, and may I share it with others who still sit in darkness. I thank You for lifting me up when I fall and for shining when my world is dark.

The Power of Life

*L*ife is such a miracle! The time from conception to birth is amazing, beyond anyone's ability to explain. Birth is followed by incredible growth in the first year, when those tiny, helpless babies figure out smiling, rolling over, sitting up, crawling, even walking. And growth continues throughout our lives—from toddler- to adulthood.

The various stages of human life—conception, birth, growth, and maturity—occur in our faith life, too, as God mysteriously plants a seed in our hearts, bringing us to the point of spiritual birth. Then we take the faltering steps of spiritual toddlerhood, drinking the milk of the Word, until we're mature enough to handle the meat of the scripture.

We as educators see a similar growth cycle in our students. Their learning proceeds from letters to words to paragraphs, from numerals to simple addition to algebra, from memorizing names, dates, and places to understanding how those various facts fit the context of history. Education is another amazing journey of life—one we're privileged to be a part of.

Whether in the physical, spiritual, or intellectual life, there must be a source of nurture that enables growth to occur. In the faith life, what is that source of nurture? John 15 pictures a vine (Jesus Himself) that supplies branches (us as Christians) with everything necessary to grow and bear fruit.

Isn't it interesting that branches don't labor to bear their fruit? The fruit is a spontaneous result of the life that flows through the branch from the nurturing vine. And it's prayer that keeps that spiritual "sap" flowing. We talk directly with God, sharing our concerns, seeking His guidance, giving thanks for His help, and honoring His presence in our lives. We commune with Him from deep inside, touching His life and allowing Him to touch ours.

Let's seek ways of keeping that life connection open. It can be a challenge for us as teachers, with the demands of our students, colleagues, and families. We don't have leisurely hours to sit at Jesus' feet like the biblical Mary, no matter how much we might want to. Most of us will only be able to carve out a brief time for Bible reading and prayer each day. But as we make the Lord our priority, He'll reveal ways for us to pursue a deeper relationship with Him. Always remember: God desires our company—why else would He have sent Jesus to die for our sins?

As teachers, let's avoid the temptation to view prayer as just another item on an already too full to-do list. Instead, let's see it as an opportunity to become more intimately acquainted with our heavenly Father. That relationship makes everything else in life possible.

Abiding in the Vine

"I am the vine, you are the branches; he who abides in Me and I in him, he bears much fruit, for apart from Me you can do nothing."
JOHN 15:5 NASB

*L*ord Jesus, You are the source of my life. My connection to You is very real, and I depend on You for everything. I want to be a healthy branch, growing and bearing fruit. Thank You for this life relationship, Lord. May I remain in You throughout this day, so that every thought I think, every word I speak, every prayer I pray comes from You.

The Father's Gift

"For God so loved the world that he gave his one and only Son, that whoever believes in him shall not perish but have eternal life."
JOHN 3:16 NIV

*F*ather, may I never take this verse for granted! Because it's so familiar, I sometimes forget the depth of love it represents: the precious gift of Your only Son, the opportunity I have to believe in Him, and ultimately, eternal life. Let me live before others in a way so they, too, can believe and live forever! May I freely share the gift of Your Son and the life He gives.

Life and Peace
*For the mind set on the flesh is death,
but the mind set on the Spirit is life and peace.*
ROMANS 8:6 NASB

*L*ord Jesus, what a wonderful promise this is! As I give You control over who I am, I can experience life and peace. How I need that in the daily whirl of teaching! Keep me close to You in prayer, and help me set my mind on You alone. Turn me from myself and the world around me, Lord. Help me yield to Your Spirit's control as I teach and love my students today.

Bread of Life
*Then Jesus declared, "I am the bread of life. He who comes to me will never
go hungry, and he who believes in me will never be thirsty."*
JOHN 6:35 NIV

*D*ear Bread of Life, I come to you, hungry in my soul. You always fill me—You never leave me wanting. The physical food I eat lasts only so long. Even the facts I teach my students may soon be forgotten. But You are a full and eternal portion, Lord. I thank You that I can eat this bread today. Thank You for satisfying my deepest needs.

The Spirit Gives Life

He has made us competent as ministers of a new covenant—not of the letter but of the Spirit; for the letter kills, but the Spirit gives life.

2 CORINTHIANS 3:6 NIV

O Lord, let me share Your life with those around me. Not a list of rules and regulations, Lord, but the peaceful, joyful, loving life You've promised. May I enliven my friends, coworkers, and students as I minister this new covenant, offering Your Spirit rather than the law. I thank You for the freedom of this faith life.

Resurrection and Life

Jesus said to her, "I am the resurrection and the life. He who believes in me will live, even though he dies; and whoever lives and believes in me will never die. Do you believe this?"

JOHN 11:25–26 NIV

*L*ord Jesus, I'll say, like Martha, that I believe! It's amazing— You not only raised the dead; You are resurrection itself. You are *life*. I can't really understand it, but I believe it, Lord. What hope I have, knowing I'll enjoy an eternal life and never die! Help me to share this wonderful truth with someone today.

The Narrow Way

"Enter through the narrow gate; for the gate is wide and the way is broad that leads to destruction, and there are many who enter through it."
MATTHEW 7:13 NASB

*D*ear Lord, I want to be one of the few who find the small gate and the narrow way, which lead to life. Please help me find others going that way, too, so we can share the journey together, both now and in eternity.

Hidden in Christ

Set your minds on things above, not on earthly things. For you died, and your life is now hidden with Christ in God.
COLOSSIANS 3:2–3 NIV

*L*ord, how often I act as if my life was all about the details of my schedule. The truth is that my life is in You. Today, Father, I want to focus on the "things above." Let me dwell there, and may the peace You give be a testimony to others of what life is truly about. Thank You for this safe place, where I am hidden in You.

Water of Life

The Spirit and the bride say, "Come!" And let him who hears say, "Come!" Whoever is thirsty, let him come; and whoever wishes, let him take the free gift of the water of life.
REVELATION 22:17 NIV

*L*ord Jesus, I thank You for the free gift of the water of life. I never have to thirst again! Please help me share this living water with others who are still thirsty, so that many more can be part of this bride who longs for Your return. Come, Lord Jesus!

The Gift of God

For the wages of sin is death, but the free gift
of God is eternal life in Christ Jesus our Lord.
ROMANS 6:23 NASB

*F*ather, I am awed by the gift of eternal life You gave through Your Son. What a contrast—death and life. Please help me share this gift of life with those in my school, showing them the way out of death. I thank You for this wonderful gift You've offered us so freely through Your Son's death on the cross.

Christ Lives in Me

"I have been crucified with Christ; and it is no longer I who live, but Christ
lives in me; and the life which I now live in the flesh I live by faith in the
Son of God, who loved me and gave Himself up for me."
GALATIANS 2:20 NASB

*D*ear Lord, what freedom this is! I don't even live anymore—it's You living in me. Please help me realize that You've done the work. I have only to enjoy the benefits of Your labors. May I freely share this life with others, Lord.

Eternal Life in the Son

And this is the testimony: God has given us eternal life, and this
life is in his Son. He who has the Son has life; he who does
not have the Son of God does not have life.

1 JOHN 5:11–12 NIV

*F*ather, I thank You for giving us eternal life in Your Son.
I praise You for Your marvelous gift through Him. Some
say there are many ways to reach You, but Your Word
shows clearly that eternal life is only through Jesus. May
I be bold today to share this truth.

A Fragrance of Christ

For we are a fragrance of Christ to God among those who are being saved
and among those who are perishing; to the one an aroma from death to
death, to the other an aroma from life to life.

2 CORINTHIANS 2:15–16 NASB

*L*ord Jesus, fill me with Yourself so that others around
me will "smell" You. I want to take You in and breathe
You out as an aroma of life! May Your fragrance perme-
ate my classroom today, bringing my students and fellow
teachers into Your life.

Laying Down Our Lives

This is how we know what love is: Jesus Christ laid down his life for us. And we ought to lay down our lives for our brothers.
1 JOHN 3:16 NIV

*D*ear Lord, what an example You set in laying Your life down for us. Your love for us cost You so much. May I be willing to lay down my life for others, too. May I hold my own thoughts, opinions, and desires loosely, giving them up when necessary to show love to others.

The Power of Vision

*N*obody becomes a teacher to get rich. Maybe at the college level or the high end of public school administration, the salaries are more impressive, but most of us don't hold those positions. The majority of teachers have a reasonable income, probably with a good health plan as a fringe benefit.

But income is only a small part of the reason we teach. Most of us are *called* to teach. We teach because we must—because we have a vision.

We have pursued teaching from a deep desire to make a difference in the world. We truly hold the next generation in our hands. Next to the home, the classroom probably has the most influence upon the growing minds and hearts of young people.

For many of us, a teacher's influence sparked the passion to teach others. The words or actions of one particular person probably made a lifelong impression upon us. Maybe that teacher prayed each day to make a difference—and God used that educator to shape our destiny.

Some of us follow a family tradition in our teaching. For some older teachers, especially women, teaching was one of a handful of career choices they could pursue.

Whatever the reasons we entered the field, we all share a love for young people and a passion for helping others.

Georgina Smith is a woman with that kind of drive. She left a twenty-year career as a corporate executive "to do something more meaningful and fulfilling with my life," she wrote in the September 2006 edition of *Guideposts* magazine. Every night, Smith saw kids watching television, playing video games, and generally goofing around at a local Laundromat. Thinking they could use their time more beneficially, she began carrying crates of books to the place three times a week.

Not only did the kids begin reading, they also discussed what they read—among themselves and with their parents. Smith expanded her "library" to several other locations and invited education students from a nearby college to help tutor. These prospective teachers have had the privilege of experiencing Georgina's "outside-the-box" thinking, as well as making a difference in the lives of children.

What motivates Georgina Smith? The knowledge that she has an opportunity to change children's lives every day. That's the vision that keeps most of us going, whether we run an innovative program like Georgina Smith's or simply explain ordinary things like multiplication tables and verb tenses.

A Hopeful Vision

Where there is no vision, the people perish:
but he that keepeth the law, happy is he.
PROVERBS 29:18 KJV

*L*ord, we would surely perish if we didn't have the vision of Your plan for our lives as teachers. You brought us to this position, You supply us for our duties each day, and You will accomplish Your desire through us wherever we work. I thank You that I can trust You in the good times—when the job is going smoothly—as well as those times when Your design is less clear. Give me a vision, Lord—of You and of what You're accomplishing through me.

He Is Faithful

Faithful is He who calls you, and He also will bring it to pass.
1 THESSALONIANS 5:24 NASB

*L*ord Jesus, You are the faithful One. I can trust You to accomplish Your will through me as I interact with my students and other people at school. I believe You called me to be a teacher, even as You called me to salvation. You'll never leave me alone—You'll always see me through. Lord, You lived a faithful life Yourself, doing whatever the Father set before You. May I live faithfully, as well.

Faithful Obedience

*By faith Abraham, when called to go to a place he would
later receive as his inheritance, obeyed and went,
even though he did not know where he was going.*

HEBREWS 11:8 NIV

*F*ather, sometimes I feel like Abraham—as if I'm striking
out blindly, not knowing where You're leading. But I know
that You are faithful and I can trust You. Help me in my
unbelief, Lord, and keep me looking to You—for direction
today and for my eternal inheritance. May I leave a legacy
of obedience even as Abraham did.

A Worthy Life

*As a prisoner for the Lord, then, I urge you to
live a life worthy of the calling you have received.*

EPHESIANS 4:1 NIV

*L*ord Jesus, what an honor it is to be Your prisoner! I'm
not locked up in jail as the apostle Paul often was, but I'm
enslaved by love to You. You have called me to faith—and
to my vocation as an educator. I take them both seriously
and want to live a life worthy of these callings. I thank
You, Lord, that You empower me to do both.

All Things Working Together

And we know that God causes all things to work together for good to those who love God, to those who are called according to His purpose.
ROMANS 8:28 NASB

*L*ord, I thank You for this promise. I trust that You are working, especially when little in life makes sense. Sometimes, when the day falls apart and I feel like crying, I know I can turn to You and whisper an "amen" in my heart. In Your faithful care, I can trust that even the bad days are in Your hands. Please teach me new lessons of faith, Father.

Pressing On
I press toward the mark for the prize of
the high calling of God in Christ Jesus.
PHILIPPIANS 3:14 KJV

*F*ather, You created me with a desire always to reach forward, to strive to attain something in this life. Often I reach for things that aren't true prizes but mere shadows of the real prize. Your calling, Lord, is the highest goal to which I can attain—it overshadows all the awards and honors I can earn in my profession. Please keep me focused today on the real goal—of gaining Christ.

Called into Fellowship
God, who has called you into fellowship with
his Son Jesus Christ our Lord, is faithful.
1 CORINTHIANS 1:9 NIV

*F*ather, what a blessed place to be—in fellowship with Your Son, Jesus Christ. Here I can pour out my heart in praise for all You've done and for all You are doing in my life. Here I can bring my concerns about my students, my job, and everything else I find important. Here I can intercede for those You have put on my heart, knowing You will hear and answer. Here I can learn to know You, the faithful God.

God's Guiding Hand

*If I take the wings of the dawn, if I dwell in the remotest
part of the sea, even there Your hand will lead me,
and Your right hand will lay hold of me.*

PSALM 139:9–10 NASB

*F*ather, what a precious psalm this is! Wherever I go, You are with me—at home, in my classroom, anywhere. In the best circumstances or the worst, You promise to hold me and protect me. In light of such love, Lord, may I never complain or fear.

Put into Service

*I thank Christ Jesus our Lord, who has strengthened me, because He
considered me faithful, putting me into service.*

1 TIMOTHY 1:12 NASB

*L*ord Jesus, I thank You for the reminder that I am in Your service and that You strengthen me for the task. Some days it all seems too much; I wonder why I'm in this field, but I want to be found faithful, Lord. I believe You have called me to teach and put me right where I am. Energize me, Lord, physically and spiritually, to carry out Your service.

The Gift of Teaching

*We have different gifts, according to the grace given us. If a man's gift. . .
is serving, let him serve; if it is teaching, let him teach.*
ROMANS 12:6–7 NIV

*F*ather, You have given us a variety of gifts in Your body,
the church. As teachers, we recognize that our ability is
a gift from You, and we want to use it to bring glory to
You. We want to teach according to the grace You give.
We desire to be Your hands, reaching out to others, and
Your mouth, speaking truth and life.

Our Real Calling

*That you would walk worthy of God who
calls you into His own kingdom and glory.*
1 THESSALONIANS 2:12 NKJV

*D*ear Lord, this is my true calling: walking worthily into
Your kingdom and glory. My calling as a teacher is but a
reflection of Your highest priority. May I order my steps
in such a way as to be worthy of Your calling, spiritually
and professionally. Help me, Father, to show Your life
within me to the world outside. May it be clear to those
around me that You are the Lord of my life.

His Calling

With this in mind, we constantly pray for you, that our God may count
you worthy of his calling, and that by his power he may fulfill every good
purpose of yours and every act prompted by your faith.

2 THESSALONIANS 1:11 NIV

*D*ear Lord, we need to pray for one another even as the saints of the New Testament constantly interceded for one another. Help me to pray—for myself and my fellow teachers—that we would be faithful to live as believers in our schools and communities. Each of us needs Your power to carry out the tasks You give us to fulfill.

Called According to His Purpose

Who has saved us and called us with a holy calling, not according
to our works, but according to His own purpose and grace which
was granted us in Christ Jesus from all eternity.

2 TIMOTHY 1:9 NASB

*D*ear God, I thank You that our calling is not dependent upon our own efforts, but upon Your purpose and the grace You gave us in Jesus. Your purpose is never random but something You've planned for all time. I want to be one with Your plan—one with You in Your eternal purpose of bringing people to know You.

The Faithful Slave

"Who then is the faithful and sensible slave whom his
master put in charge of his household to give them their
food at the proper time? Blessed is that slave whom his
master finds so doing when he comes."
MATTHEW 24:45–46 NASB

*L*ord Jesus, I want to be a faithful "slave," doing the
right job at the right time. In my teaching, Lord, may
I give instruction, discipline, guidance, or correction to
my students at the most appropriate moments. Please
give me the sensitivity to carry out this task, Lord.
Strengthen me today so I may be found faithful.

The Power of Acceptance

Undoubtedly, you're familiar with *Mr. Rogers' Neighborhood*. Depending on your age, you either grew up with the PBS classic or raised your children on it. Fred Rogers taught millions of children through the television, often sharing his grandfather's sentiment, "There's only one person in this world like you—and I like you exactly as you are." What an example of unconditional acceptance!

As teachers, we have the opportunity to convey that message to our students, so they can live their own lives free from the pressure to conform to others' expectations. Those of us who have been accepted by a loving heavenly Father have His life-changing love to share. And our students need it.

Of course, acceptance doesn't mean license. We don't say "anything goes," or we'd have chaos in our classrooms. Finding the right balance is a matter of daily prayer as we seek the Lord's wisdom.

But we need to affirm our kids simply for who they are, encouraging them to pursue their legitimate interests and dreams. We don't want to be like the art teacher who advised Theodore Geisel against a career in art. Fortunately, "Dr. Seuss" ignored those words. "What does an artist look like?" he asked. "He may be the one you least expect to succeed because he follows the beat of a different drummer."

What a challenge in a classroom with twenty or thirty drummers! But with plenty of patience and prayer, the Lord can help us create trust with our students through our words and actions. As we endeavor to meet our pupils' needs, God will guide us to hear and nurture each different drummer we meet.

I believe in you. You're special. I like you. I'm listening. These are powerful messages we can say or live out loud with our students. Each day we can pray for opportunities to encourage them, giving them room to try new things. Sure, they'll fail sometimes. But they'll also learn and grow throughout the process.

It would be wonderful to be remembered by our students the way a woman named Roberta remembers her junior high home economics teacher: "She made me feel noticed for what I was inside." That's unconditional love and acceptance, very much like what Jesus offers each of us. As we pray, let's ask God to help us give this gift to our students.

Accepted by Christ

Accept one another, then, just as Christ
accepted you, in order to bring praise to God.
ROMANS 15:7 NIV

*D*ear Jesus, I thank You for the way You accept me—just as I am. I don't have to clean up my act to win Your approval. May I treat others the same way, Lord. It's easy to accept those nice students who cooperate. But others, the ones who don't fit the mold? Surely they need to feel appreciation as much as the others, maybe even more. Enlarge my heart, Father, to make a place for them, too—just as they are.

Welcoming Jesus

"And whoever welcomes a little child like this in my name welcomes me."
MATTHEW 18:5 NIV

*D*ear Lord, each day I have the opportunity to welcome You into my classroom—as the students who walk through my doors. They don't always "look" like You, Lord—they talk about things they shouldn't, they give each other trouble, and they create disturbances. But You've told me to welcome them as if I were welcoming You. May my students sense Your love in my words and actions and feel truly welcome.

Gentleness in Evidence

Let your gentleness be evident to all. The Lord is near.
PHILIPPIANS 4:5 NIV

*D*ear Jesus, You modeled gentleness as You lived on this earth. You dealt with all kinds of people, considering their true situation and the condition of their hearts, without ever being demanding. Today, within me, You'll enable me to interact with others in the same way. May I be willing to put myself aside, empowered by Your Spirit to love and serve others.

Bearing with One Another

Be completely humble and gentle; be patient,
bearing with one another in love.

EPHESIANS 4:2 NIV

*L*ord Jesus, I confess there is nothing humble, gentle, or patient about me most days. I plow through the classroom door with my agenda in mind, demanding that people get busy so we can "get it all done." But with that mind-set, how can I show forbearance? Being "completely humble and gentle" is exactly what I need to make a difference in my classroom, Lord. Change me so that others will see You in my life.

A New Heart

So, as those who have been chosen of God, holy and beloved, put on a heart of
compassion, kindness, humility, gentleness and patience; bearing with one
another, and forgiving each other, whoever has a complaint against anyone;
just as the Lord forgave you, so also should you.

COLOSSIANS 3:12–13 NASB

*F*ather, please show Your virtues through my life. Dress me in Your righteous robes today—my own clothes are dirty and torn, stained by sin. But You are changing me from the inside out, reaching others with compassion, kindness, humility, gentleness, and patience. May Your fruit in my life make a genuine difference in all my relationships.

The Least of These

"The King will reply, 'I tell you the truth, whatever you did for one of the least of these brothers of mine, you did for me.'"
MATTHEW 25:40 NIV

*L*ord Jesus, it's so hard to treat each student lovingly. But it's so necessary. I know, Lord, that those students who are the hardest to love usually need it the most. I don't relish hugging a porcupine, Father, but please strengthen me to reach out even to the "prickly" people. And may I never forget the quiet children, those with special learning needs, and those who are just different. Touch them all through me today.

Transformed, Not Conformed

And do not be conformed to this world, but be transformed by the renewing of your mind, that you may prove what is that good and acceptable and perfect will of God.
ROMANS 12:2 NKJV

*D*ear Jesus, may my life reflect Your transforming work as You renew my mind. Help me show my students that it's okay to be different, when that means being like You. You, Lord—not some popular singer or actor—are the Person we should aspire to be like. May my character—and those of my students—be made new by You.

God Looks at the Heart

"Do not look at his appearance or at the height of his stature...
for God sees not as man sees, for man looks at the outward
appearance, but the LORD looks at the heart."
1 SAMUEL 16:7 NASB

Lord, it's true that I can't see into my students' hearts. But please keep me from only looking at their outward appearance. Give me Your eyes to see past their words and behaviors to the people they really are—hurting, needy, and hungry for Your love. Pour that love through me, Father, to bring these students to healing.

Forgiveness

Be kind and compassionate to one another, forgiving each other,
just as in Christ God forgave you.
EPHESIANS 4:32 NIV

*L*ord Jesus, Your forgiveness is complete. You removed my sins as far as the east is from the west—and You tell me to extend the same forgiveness to others. That's a tough one, Lord—I want to argue, *You don't know what that person did!* But You do know. How can I not forgive? How can I not show Your kindness and compassion to others, forgiving every offense even as I've been forgiven?

The Fruit of the Spirit

But the fruit of the Spirit is love, joy, peace, patience, kindness, goodness,
faithfulness, gentleness, self-control; against such things there is no law.
GALATIANS 5:22–23 NASB

*L*ord, fruit grows spontaneously, not by its own effort. I want to bear Your fruit, not of my own work but as a supernatural result of Your Spirit filling me. What a contrast, Lord—the fruit of my effort versus the fruit of Your life within me. May my words, my actions, and my reactions today all show Your presence in my life. May they all manifest You!

Harmonious Living

To sum up, all of you be harmonious, sympathetic,
brotherly, kindhearted, and humble in spirit.
1 PETER 3:8 NASB

*F*ather, we as Your children often make a noise that is not pleasant or harmonious. But You want our living to reflect Your loving nature. Like an orchestra playing in tune together, may we interact with one another to make a "joyful noise" for the world to hear. May we demonstrate sincere sympathy, kindness, and humility as You fill us, touching others amid the discord so prominent in our schools and society.

Love Never Fails

Love is patient, love is kind. It does not envy, it does not boast,
it is not proud. It is not rude, it is not self-seeking, it is not easily
angered, it keeps no record of wrongs. Love does not delight in evil
but rejoices with the truth. It always protects, always trusts,
always hopes, always perseveres. Love never fails.
1 CORINTHIANS 13:4–8 NIV

*F*ather, only You can love like this. So I ask You to fill me with that kind of love. It is able to meet every situation I will face today. Your love can help me accept— unconditionally—every student I teach. I thank You, Lord, for loving through me.

Being Receptive

*"He who receives you receives Me, and he who
receives Me receives Him who sent Me."*
MATTHEW 10:40 NASB

*F*ather God, to receive someone else is to receive Jesus—
and therefore to receive You. It's like a test of our love
to see how accepting we are. I don't want to close my
arms to my students. May I give them a reception that
reflects my love for You and Your love for each of us. My
open door may be the lifeline a young person desperately
needs to know someone cares.

A Renewed Mind

*Be of the same mind toward one another; do not be haughty in mind, but
associate with the lowly. Do not be wise in your own estimation.*
ROMANS 12:16 NASB

*L*ord Jesus, renew my thoughts by replacing them with
Yours. When disagreements arise, may I be the first to
drop my opinion and listen to other people's ideas. May
I not be proud, insisting that things go my way. May I
not hold myself up above others but learn from everyone
around me. Please change me from being a "know-it-all"
to a person who yields to Your way.

My Room

The Power of Hospitality

*W*hat a challenge is set before us—to create an environment in which students can feel comfortable yet also challenged to grow and develop. Providing for the educational, social, and spiritual needs of our students is a huge task. We need to bathe every aspect of our classroom in prayer—from the physical details to the unseen, but real, atmosphere in our school space.

The director of one major child-care facility considers the environment of the classroom by putting herself in the child's position. When she looks through the classroom door, she inspects it to see what kind of welcome the class will get. She likes to see everything facing the class, welcoming them to their new room. That feeling is important so students know they are appreciated in the class, no matter what their previous level of academic excellence. Students who feel accepted are more likely to succeed.

Those of us in the public venue have to find subtle ways to incorporate our faith. Part of our testimony can be to create a warm and inviting space that helps facilitate learning and meets our students' emotional needs.

Because, as Christians, we value each human life, we can let students know they are important by:

- helping our students from other countries feel welcome to both our class and our country;
- helping shy and quiet students find a voice;
- making sure that in our school no child is bullied or treated in any other abusive way; and
- helping our students learn positive social skills that will make them better students, better members of society, and better citizens.

With the Lord's help and regular prayer for the members of our classes, we can create an atmosphere in which each child feels important, needed, and welcome.

Practice Hospitality

Share with God's people who are in need. Practice hospitality.
ROMANS 12:13 NIV

*D*ear Lord, I want my classroom to be a safe haven. I know that I don't have all the answers, so the apostle Paul's word *practice* really describes what I'm doing—working, as best I can, to create a warm atmosphere that will make my students feel loved. They come with needs both large and small. I can't begin to meet all those needs, Lord, but at least I can be a channel of Your grace, letting them know there is a place where someone truly cares.

Creating a Special Room

"Let's make a small room on the roof and put in it a bed and a table, a chair and a lamp for him. Then he can stay there whenever he comes to us."
2 KINGS 4:10 NIV

*L*ord, just as the Shunammite woman prepared a small room for Elisha, I want to create a special place for my students. Increase my sensitivity so I can know what their deepest needs are; then guide me to meet them. Please help me make a place that will let them know how important they are—to me and to You.

Doing Good

Do not withhold good from those who deserve it,
when it is in your power to act.

PROVERBS 3:27 NIV

*L*ord Jesus, the term do-gooder has a negative connotation, but I know You reach others through the good deeds You lead me to perform. No matter how busy I am, please help me to make time to help those You've brought into my life. Keep me from holding too tightly to my time or possessions when You call me to share them.

Devoted to Doing Good

This is a trustworthy saying. And I want you to stress these things, so
that those who have trusted in God may be careful to devote themselves to
doing what is good. These things are excellent and profitable for everyone.

TITUS 3:8 NIV

*F*ather, we want those we encounter each day to be better for having crossed our paths. Not richer or wiser, but different because they have touched You through us. Help me to speak kind words and perform loving deeds, so that everybody wins. May I be devoted to doing good.

An Open Door

*"But no stranger had to spend the night in the street,
for my door was always open to the traveler."*
JOB 31:32 NIV

*F*ather, I want to have open doors for everyone You bring my way. May the doors of my classroom—and of my heart—be open to friends and strangers alike. May no one ever feel lonely or burdened because my door was closed to them. Use my classroom as a way station for those traveling through my school building—and my life.

A Cup of Cold Water

*"And whoever in the name of a disciple gives to one of
these little ones even a cup of cold water to drink,
truly I say to you, he shall not lose his reward."*
MATTHEW 10:42 NASB

*L*ord Jesus, make me a dispenser of cups of cold water to those thirsty ones in need of refreshing. I am surrounded by "little ones" with needs. Many times it's only a small gesture on my part, but it can be such a life-changing act when done in Your name. Thank You, Lord, for the privilege of serving these students.

Pleasing Sacrifices

*And do not neglect doing good and sharing,
for with such sacrifices God is pleased.*
HEBREWS 13:16 NASB

*L*ord, I want to offer sacrifices that please You. Just as I'm delighted when students obey me, may I, as Your child, please You by investing in the lives of others. It is truly a sacrifice, Lord, when I have so many other things that need to be done. Work through my selfish nature, Father, motivating me by Your Spirit to reach out to others.

Entertaining Angels

*Do not neglect to show hospitality to strangers, for by this
some have entertained angels without knowing it.*
HEBREWS 13:2 NASB

*L*ord, the thought of angels among us is amazing, especially when I consider that the most difficult student might be hiding a set of wings behind his back. May I love the unlovely as if You were in their place, because it might be that You sent them—angels in my classroom—without my knowing it.

Reaping a Harvest

*Let us not become weary in doing good, for at the
proper time we will reap a harvest if we do not give up.*
GALATIANS 6:9 NIV

*L*ord Jesus, You are our model for perseverance. You never gave up, even when facing death on the cross. You'll probably never call me to such suffering, but I do get tired and discouraged in the daily grind. Sometimes I feel like giving up, Lord. Strengthen me to keep going, faithfully sowing seeds as I teach, trusting You for the harvest.

No Grumbling

Offer hospitality to one another without grumbling.
1 PETER 4:9 NIV

*D*ear Lord, that's an impossible command, but I thank You that I don't have to rely on my own strength to be hospitable. If it were up to me, many days I'd tell everyone to go away and leave me alone. But You've put me here to accomplish Your good will, Lord. May I not grumble or complain, even when I've been treated unfairly. May I glorify You in my gracious service, which You enable me to do.

Cheerful Givers

Each man should give what he has decided in his heart to give, not reluctantly or under compulsion, for God loves a cheerful giver.
2 CORINTHIANS 9:7 NIV

O Lord, I want to be a cheerful giver. Not the kind of person who grits teeth and clenches fists while grudgingly parting with time and possessions. No! I want to be the one who smiles and sincerely says, "Sure, I'd be happy to!" Put Your generous spirit in me, Lord. Make me a cheerful giver!

The Gift of Giving

We have different gifts, according to the grace given us. If a man's gift. . . is contributing to the needs of others, let him give generously.
ROMANS 12:6, 8 NIV

*L*ord Jesus, not everyone has the gift of giving, but in this profession, we all need to be givers. We are called upon to give time, energy, care, and support. For some of my teacher friends, giving comes easily. For others, it's more of a challenge. May I learn from each one, accepting that we give in different ways and amounts, according to the grace You've given us.

The Caring Samaritan

"But a certain Samaritan, as he journeyed, came where he was. And when he saw him, he had compassion. So he went to him and bandaged his wounds, pouring on oil and wine; and he set him on his own animal, brought him to an inn, and took care of him."
LUKE 10:33–34 NKJV

*D*ear Lord, make us all caring Samaritans—those who notice when others have been hurt then come near to care for their wounds. Even when it costs me something—time or energy or money—may I never be afraid to get involved, to bring a healing touch, to make a difference.

Open Hands

"For the poor will never cease to be in the land; therefore I command you, saying, 'You shall freely open your hand to your brother, to your needy and poor in your land.'"
DEUTERONOMY 15:11 NASB

*F*ather, just as You gave Your Son freely, may I extend open hands to others, giving of myself and my possessions to meet their needs. I can't fix many of my students' problems, but may I never use that as an excuse to remain inactive. Show me today, Lord, what little step I can take to help another. May our collective small steps make a big difference.

My School

The Power of Belonging

*A*t home, at school, or at work, everyone needs to feel a sense of belonging. Being left out is one of the loneliest feelings in the world. Children can detect insincerity the minute they walk in the door, so our efforts to create a warm environment in our schools must be genuine. An inviting school environment goes beyond the classroom setting and requires coordination among teachers and staff. As we seek to reach that goal, prayer certainly makes a difference, for it helps us desire to have a building where students feel at home and gives us the ability to make it happen.

One teacher recalled how even the janitors at his school befriended him when he was growing up. He also remembers teachers who influenced him, creating an overall feeling that school was a good place to be.

We often hear, "I felt so at home," about a school where the staff truly works to make students feel welcome. That atmosphere takes a lot of work and prayer to create. It may be a conscious effort based on a negative experience—possibly our own, when we felt we weren't included or that we didn't belong. Such a life lesson can make us determined that all children who walk through our doors will know they have a place in our classrooms and in our hearts.

Many teachers and administrators see the damage bullies cause. One study showed that a third of young children were afraid to even go to the restroom, because they might encounter a bully. As a result, teachers are being taught how to deal with bullying behavior and work with students to create safe environments. As these efforts succeed, everyone will win, including the bullies. When we add prayer to new rules and training, the changes will have an even greater effect.

We need to ask, "What happens when new students enter our schools? What happens when language is an issue?" A smile is understood universally, so that is the best way to begin. Then add lots of patience and understanding. Imagine yourself in their position, and help your students do the same. A little encouragement to understand a new person's situation can help everyone learn to be more compassionate, creating the kind of atmosphere we all desire.

The invisible sign above our school door should read ALL ARE WELCOME HERE, and our efforts to convey this should be visible, creating a tangible feeling of belonging. Let's pray together about how to make our welcome real.

The Shadow of His Wings

How precious is Your lovingkindness, O God! Therefore the children of men put their trust under the shadow of Your wings.

PSALM 36:7 NKJV

O Lord, Your love for us is amazing! We belong to You and are safe in Your care. Let us offer a similar security to our students, who desperately need someone to care. Like chicks who hide under the hen's wings, may they feel safe in our building, a shelter in the storms they face. May our hearts and our rooms be havens for those who need a safe place, for those who need You.

Many Members

For the body is not one member, but many.

1 CORINTHIANS 12:14 NASB

*F*ather, how wonderfully You made our bodies and what a picture they are of coordination. We long for our schools to function in the same way, with each member performing a different job, working together with all the other members for the good of the whole.

Our Value

"Are not two sparrows sold for a cent? And yet not one of them will fall to the ground apart from your Father. But the very hairs of your head are all numbered. So do not fear; you are more valuable than many sparrows."
MATTHEW 10:29–31 NASB

*F*ather, how precious to realize our value in Your sight. You care more than we realize for each of us and for our students, as well. May our building be a place where this kind of value is evident—that each of us is of infinite value to our Creator and therefore to one another.

Laboring Together

Two are better than one, because they have a good reward for their labor. For if they fall, one will lift up his companion. But woe to him who is alone when he falls, for he has no one to help him up.
ECCLESIASTES 4:9–10 NKJV

O Lord, surely we need to labor together as teachers. Some days we fall down and need someone to help us to our feet. We get so tired, and the needs around us are so great. We want to be a real strength to one another, helping our coworkers and praying as we work together.

Love Fervently

*And above all things have fervent love for one another,
for "love will cover a multitude of sins."*
1 PETER 4:8 NKJV

*L*ord Jesus, give us a burning love for one another and for each of our students. In a society where people delight in uncovering private details of their lives in a tell-all fashion, help us remember that sometimes the most loving thing is to say nothing to others, to simply bring matters to You in prayer. As we pray and love others, may they see a heavenly "glow" around our words and actions, drawing them to You.

Suffering and Rejoicing Together

And if one member suffers, all the members suffer with it; if one member is honored, all the members rejoice with it.

1 CORINTHIANS 12:26 NASB

O Lord, we truly desire to be connected to this extent! But it takes time to get to know one another, and our schedules are so full. We have so many demands on our time already; how can we pursue relationships to this degree? Yet You have put us together—staff and students— for a reason. So I ask You to open my heart to make room for others' joys and sorrows.

Trusting the Lord

The LORD is good, a refuge in times of trouble. He cares for those who trust in him.

NAHUM 1:7 NIV

*D*ear Lord, how blessed we are to have a safe place in You where we can run in times of trouble. You will never turn us away, but You care for us and help us. May we represent that safety to our students, offering refuge when they need someone to talk to, someone to share the loads they carry. Care for them through us as they learn to trust, first a person then You.

We Need One Another

And the eye cannot say to the hand, "I have no need of you";
nor again the head to the feet, "I have no need of you."
1 CORINTHIANS 12:21 NKJV

*L*ord Jesus, forgive me for ever thinking someone You have placed in my life was not necessary, for this means I am not appreciating Your design. As each member of our physical body is vital to our health, each person at my school is there for a reason. May I never criticize other members but appreciate their various functions so the school can manifest Your plan through our coordinated effort.

A Refuge

The Lord is a refuge for the oppressed,
a stronghold in times of trouble.
PSALM 9:9 NIV

*F*ather, so many people in our schools are oppressed and in trouble. Some young people who walk through our doors each day have been neglected and abused; they feel unloved and unwanted. They face temptations they hardly know how to handle. Some of the teachers in rooms next to ours have children and marriages that seem hopeless. You have the answers each of them needs, the safety they desire and the strength to face another day. Help us lead them to You.

Songs of Deliverance

You are my hiding place; you will protect me from
trouble and surround me with songs of deliverance.
PSALM 32:7 NIV

*F*ather, Your protection is priceless. Everywhere we turn, there is trouble. In our personal lives, we have difficult seasons. In our professional lives, our daily schedules alone are challenging; then we have testing and extra crises that threaten to put us over the edge. But in You, we are safe. You meet us with comfort and give us songs to strengthen us and provide deliverance. May Your song be heard through our lives.

Our Dwelling Place

For you have made the LORD, my refuge,
even the Most High, your dwelling place.
PSALM 91:9 NASB

*D*ear Lord, amid so much unrest and uncertainty, to know we have a dwelling place in You brings warmth and comfort to our hearts. We rest in being loved by You, belonging to You. We are surrounded by people who need this same assurance. Make it real to us so it can become real to them. May the atmosphere we create in our classrooms and in our buildings reflect the safety of our eternal home in You.

A Cord of Three

Though one may be overpowered, two can defend themselves.
A cord of three strands is not quickly broken.
ECCLESIASTES 4:12 NIV

*L*ord Jesus, what power You add to any relationship! Alone we are weak; when we team up with another, we are stronger. But when we bring You into any relationship, it becomes nearly invincible. Keep us from being "Lone Rangers" in our schools. May we see the wisdom in being connected to one another and, together, to You, the strong testimony to our world, which needs to know the difference You make.

Brotherly Love

Let brotherly love continue.
HEBREWS 13:1 KJV

*F*ather, many people have never experienced brotherly love in their families, so this is not easy for them to relate to. Even among believers, all too often, there's no testimony, no reality of such love. How this must grieve Your heart. Yet everyone longs to experience the warmth and security of loving relationships, to feel welcome and accepted. Help us to create such a place in our classrooms, to experience love among ourselves and to share it with others.

Shepherding the Flock

He shall feed his flock like a shepherd: he shall gather the lambs with his arm, and carry them in his bosom, and shall gently lead those that are with young.
ISAIAH 40:11 KJV

*F*ather, what a precious picture: the shepherd with his sheep. We desire to interact with our students in such a way—feeding their minds as well as their hearts. Help us lead our "flocks" with gentleness and loving care. May we nourish our "lambs," helping them grow in a healthy way, tenderly carrying them along while they remain in our care.

My Colleagues

The Power of Teamwork

*W*hen I worked as a volunteer at our city's science museum, I learned a valuable lesson: There are no problems, only opportunities. If we look at each difficulty as a challenge or an opportunity to learn and grow, we will not only survive but thrive. That could be the motto of those who work on teams. For teamwork, challenging as it may be, is a necessary part of the teaching profession. As educators, we'll have many opportunities to work with others, since we report to an administrator and interact constantly with the other teachers and staff in our building.

We ask our students to learn teamwork. But let's admit it—we all know how group projects tend to go. One person does most of the work, and the others get the credit. Is it any wonder we often cringe when given a committee assignment? Sometimes it would just be easier to work alone. But there are many benefits to working on a team—when the team truly works together.

God surely has a sense of humor when He puts teams together. An unwritten rule seems to exist, dictating that we will be required to work with people who will drive us absolutely crazy—because they are either just like us or someone in our families, or they are the polar opposite.

After much prayer, we accept our committee positions—and sometimes come to feel that everyone working with us has a negative opinion about nearly everything we do. *Lord,* we find ourselves praying, *is this Your plan for committee work, to make things difficult?* But in the end, God shows us that even with the challenges, this work that caused so much trouble is in His design. We may pray more for our fellow committee members than we've prayed for any other coworker. And as we see our own spiritual growth and the benefits of the work we've done with others, we may finally realize God answered our prayers, though not as we expected.

Being Faithful in Prayer

Be joyful in hope, patient in affliction, faithful in prayer.
ROMANS 12:12 NIV

*L*ord Jesus, I want to be faithful in praying for those I work with and for our class as we work together with our students. Help me to turn to You many times during the day, bringing each situation to You. Thank You that there is no limit to the number of times I can pray, and I never get a busy signal or run out of minutes. You are always available and willing to listen and respond.

Suffering Is Not Strange

Dear friends, do not be surprised at the painful trial you are suffering,
as though something strange were happening to you. But rejoice
that you participate in the sufferings of Christ, so that you
may be overjoyed when his glory is revealed.
1 PETER 4:12–13 NIV

*L*ord Jesus, help me not to be surprised when there are problems with my coworkers. Instead, help me view such problems as opportunities to share in Your sufferings. Help me find You in each difficulty, with a view toward the greater joy to come.

Finding Rest and Security

My soul finds rest in God alone; my salvation comes from him. He alone is my rock and my salvation; he is my fortress, I will never be shaken.
PSALM 62:1–2 NIV

*L*ord Jesus, by myself I am so weary, so unsteady. But in You, I find rest and security no matter what is going on around me. When my coworkers expect more from me, I can hide in You. When the load is more than I think I can carry, I can trust that You are with me. Thank You for being such a supply!

Being Angry

"In your anger do not sin": Do not let the sun go down while you are still angry, and do not give the devil a foothold.
EPHESIANS 4:26–27 NIV

*L*ord Jesus, I thank You that Your Word does not say, "Do not be angry." In a job where I am working closely with others, that would be impossible. Help me to turn to You immediately when I am angry with a coworker, so the situation can be defused and not escalate into something ugly.

An Eternal Perspective

*For our light and momentary troubles are achieving for us
an eternal glory that far outweighs them all. So we fix our eyes
not on what is seen, but on what is unseen. For what is seen
is temporary, but what is unseen is eternal.*

2 CORINTHIANS 4:17–18 NIV

*L*ord Jesus, I want to have this perspective! When I consider the big picture, the eternal scene, my troubles are so small. May I interact with my coworkers with such a view—an eternal perspective, always remembering the unseen. What a glorious view!

Speaking Helpful Words

*Do not let any unwholesome talk come out of your mouths, but only what
is helpful for building others up according to their needs, that it may
benefit those who listen.*

EPHESIANS 4:29 NIV

*L*ord Jesus, may I learn to check with You before I open my mouth—to be sure my words are going to be helpful and build others up and benefit anyone who hears them. May none of the words I speak with my coworkers be unwholesome. I want to be a blessing to those I work with!

Being Conformed to His Likeness

And we know that in all things God works for the good of those who love him, who have been called according to his purpose. For those God foreknew he also predestined to be conformed to the likeness of his Son.

ROMANS 8:28–29 NIV

*L*ord, thank You that You use everything for Your good. You do not waste anything, and I rejoice in how You use each situation as You work Yourself into me, conforming me to the image of Your Son. Help me cooperate with You in this process as I interact with my coworkers.

Being Thankful

Give thanks in all circumstances, for this is God's will for you in Christ Jesus.

1 THESSALONIANS 5:18 NIV

*L*ord Jesus, I do not always feel thankful. Yet, in spite of my feelings, I give thanks, because Your Word says I should. Often I find that once I begin, I start to feel thankful because I see who You are. Then I am reminded that I can trust You, even when the situation does not change. I give thanks in faith, and You change my heart. Perhaps that is the greatest miracle. Thank You, Lord.

Being Properly Clothed

Therefore, as God's chosen people, holy and dearly loved,
clothe yourselves with compassion, kindness, humility, gentleness
and patience. Bear with each other and forgive whatever grievances
you may have against one another. Forgive as the Lord forgave you.
And over all these virtues put on love, which binds them
all together in perfect unity.
Colossians 3:12–14 niv

*L*ord Jesus, this is what I want to wear each day! Your character, Your very self. May I learn to abide in You to the extent that these virtues flow out of me to my coworkers and students.

Knowing Pure Joy

*Consider it pure joy, my brothers, whenever you face trials of many kinds,
because you know that the testing of your faith develops perseverance.
Perseverance must finish its work so that you may be mature
and complete, not lacking anything.*

JAMES 1:2–4 NIV

*L*ord Jesus, like my students, I am being tested. But my tests are through trials—many kinds of trials. Help me to have this view in difficulties: You are testing my faith for a reason—to develop perseverance so that I can be mature. I want to pass the test, Lord!

Loving Others

*"If you love those who love you, what credit is that to you?
Even 'sinners' love those who love them."*

LUKE 6:32 NIV

*L*ord Jesus, I want people at school to know there is something different about me because I live these verses— because I love people no matter what is in it for me, because I do good and give, not expecting anything in return. I cannot do this, but You can do it in me. Yours is a loving, giving life that reaches out to people and touches them.

The Golden Rule
"Do to others as you would have them do to you."
LUKE 6:31 NIV

*L*ord Jesus, thank You for the Golden Rule—a principle I can count on in my dealings with others at school. What a pattern: to give as I want to receive, to speak words I want to hear, to listen as I want to be heard, to teach as I would like to be taught. Let me treat my coworkers as I want to be treated, with integrity and kindness.

Praying in Secret
"But when you pray, go into your room, close the door and pray to your Father, who is unseen. Then your Father, who sees what is done in secret, will reward you."
MATTHEW 6:6 NIV

*L*ord Jesus, thank You for the privilege of meeting You privately and the relationship we are building in this secret place. I appreciate being able to share my concerns about my coworkers and my role as a teacher. Thank You for the difference prayer is making in my life.

Crying Out to the Lord

Listen to my prayer, O God, do not ignore my plea; hear me and answer me. My thoughts trouble me and I am distraught.
PSALM 55:1–2 NIV

*L*ord Jesus, thank You for this prayer of David that captures my feelings some days. When I am bothered, I know I can pray in such a way, confessing that I am upset and asking You to listen and answer. Thank You that You always hear me when I cry out to You. Thank You for sharing my load and bringing me peace.

My Field

The Power of Support

*I*n high school choir, we sang the song "No Man is an Island." This is certainly true in education. We need each other. Whether it's a simple need—to borrow a book or a marker—or a larger need—advice on how to deal with a difficult student—we need the support of our peers.

Like the "cloud of witnesses" described in Hebrews 12:1 (KJV), who encourage us to run the race of faith, support materials surround us, reminding us of those who have gone before and achieved success. Their testimonials assure us that we, too, can meet the challenge.

Encouragement is available in many forms: books, magazines, tapes, conferences. One avenue for support is the Christian Educators Association International. They offer an array of services including a prayer network and a magazine entitled *Teachers of Vision*.

One columnist in *Teaching K–8* often sounds a warning against the isolation that can develop from what he calls the "egg-crate structure" of our schools—where each of us is divided off from everyone else, lost in an individual compartment, struggling alone.

As believers, we need that connection on a spiritual

level. Praying with other teachers is a huge support and a powerful reminder that we are not alone in the fight. My friend Ginny, a special education teacher in an inner-city school, prays with a few in her building after school. They also read a psalm together when they meet. She says, "The washing in the water of the Word is so refreshing after a day in the trenches."

Sandy, a veteran elementary teacher, offers this advice to prospective teachers: "Mentor under some good teachers as you are considering your career choice so you see a complete picture of the expectations in your chosen field, level, and school system."

Other support can be found in various credentials and awards spread throughout the educational system. From graduate-level work and Highly Qualified certification to Teacher of the Year awards, opportunities abound for teachers to shine. Reading about their accomplishments can be encouraging, if we learn from them and see what is working, not if we use them to measure our inadequacies. Certainly we face a dilemma in education, being required to do more with regard to discipline and guidance—roles once filled by parents—with less money and, all too often, a lack of trust.

However, on our quest to be the best, let us not forget whom we serve. We may work hard to achieve a degree from a university and know the best methods and even have the best-behaved students in our buildings. But when we stand before the Lord, it will be His "well done" that brings us the most joy and the greatest fulfillment.

Devoted to One Another

Be devoted to one another in brotherly love;
give preference to one another in honor.
ROMANS 12:10 NASB

*L*ord Jesus, help me show this kind of care to my coworkers —from the superintendent to the maintenance worker in my building. I want to be devoted to each of them and to honor them. May I give even more honor to those who are believers, those who share a double bond of faith and vocation. For those who don't yet know You, may I care for them with an attitude that always demonstrates Your love.

Not Boasting, Challenging, or Envying

Let us not become boastful, challenging one another, envying one another.
GALATIANS 5:26 NASB

*F*ather, how often competition arises among us. We try to outperform one another, besting each other in our activities, achievements, and evaluations. What an ugly attitude—and what evil results. Forgive me for the times I've fallen into this trap. May I practice exactly the opposite in my dealings with other teachers, Lord. Help me to give compliments, show appreciation, and celebrate their accomplishments.

Burden Bearers
*Carry each other's burdens, and in this
way you will fulfill the law of Christ.*
GALATIANS 6:2 NIV

*D*ear Lord, some days I can hardly carry my own load, much less help with another's. Yet how grateful I've been when someone has helped me. May I pass on the same encouragement today, Lord. Please help me to see beyond my own situation and notice what those around me are dealing with: difficult students, family crises, or just bad days. May I be sensitive and help lighten their load. May I always see others through Your eyes.

Kindness, Compassion, and Forgiveness
*Be kind and compassionate to one another, forgiving each other,
just as in Christ God forgave you.*
EPHESIANS 4:32 NIV

*D*ear Lord, when You lived on this earth, You showed such kindness and compassion, reaching out and touching those who were suffering and meeting people's true needs. Even when You were dying, You forgave the thief beside You. Speak through me with kind, compassionate words that truly make my students, their parents, and the staff in my building know I care about them. Help me show them that You love them, Lord.

Love and Good Deeds

*And let us consider how we may spur one
another on toward love and good deeds.*
HEBREWS 10:24 NIV

*L*ord, this is a precious challenge—to encourage one
another to love, and to show love in our actions. I
often need help to continue caring for my challenging students or to continue offering kind words and
comfort to discouraged colleagues. But we all like a
good contest, Lord. May we work together to win the
prize, seeing who can offer the most encouragement
and the most love, in Jesus' name.

A New Heart

So, as those who have been chosen of God, holy and beloved, put on a heart of compassion, kindness, humility, gentleness and patience.

COLOSSIANS 3:12 NASB

*L*ord Jesus, when You live in my heart, all these virtues will flow out spontaneously. It's not a way of life I can create on my own. I can't pretend, either, Lord. But I can let You change who I am by Your divine life—real change that touches others. May my students and coworkers sense something different about me, Lord. May they recognize that You, also, want to do the same in them.

Conversations of Grace

Let your conversation be always full of grace, seasoned with salt, so that you may know how to answer everyone.

COLOSSIANS 4:6 NIV

O Lord, I talk so much. I instruct and interact all day— with my students, their parents, fellow teachers, other staff members, my family. So many conversations, so many opportunities to minister words which are full of grace. Just as salt makes food taste better, may my words be agreeable, bringing peace to those around me. May they reflect Your wisdom, Lord. Please guide my tongue.

Words of Grace

Do not let any unwholesome talk come out of your mouths,
but only what is helpful for building others up according to their needs,
that it may benefit those who listen.

EPHESIANS 4:29 NIV

*L*ord Jesus, please teach me to consult You before I open my mouth. I want to be sure the words I'm about to speak are good words, words which will build up, meet others' needs, and give grace. My words need to be Your words, Father. I know that everyone needs encouragement, so please touch others through the words I speak today.

Suffering and Rejoicing Together

If one member suffers, all the members suffer with it;
if one member is honored, all the members rejoice with it.

1 CORINTHIANS 12:26 NASB

*L*ord, there's so much suffering around me. I can't fix other people's situations, but surely I can show compassion for what they're going through. Help me, Lord, to spend time with others so I know their joys and sorrows. Help me to be open and vulnerable with them. Make me willing to involve myself with others—in the good times and the bad. I know, Father, that's an eternal investment.

Real Encouragement

And we urge you, brothers, warn those who are idle,
encourage the timid, help the weak, be patient with everyone.
1 THESSALONIANS 5:14 NIV

Lord Jesus, may I have this kind of influence where I work. May I encourage that new teacher who's afraid to ask for help. May I help those experiencing physical or emotional weaknesses, who struggle just to make it through each day. May I stop to consider what others are dealing with in their classes or at home, and may I offer them the same patient understanding I desire.

Barnabas in Antioch

When he arrived and saw the evidence of the grace of God, he was glad and
encouraged them all to remain true to the Lord with all their hearts.
ACTS 11:23 NIV

Dear Lord, how contagious joy and encouragement can be. When we see the many proofs of Your grace around us, may we rejoice together. The victories that come through our prayers, the changes in behavior that can only be the result of Your intervention, the strength You give to get through difficulties. These encourage us to remain faithful—and to keep praying.

Encouragement and Hope

For everything that was written in the past was written to teach us,
so that through endurance and the encouragement
of the Scriptures we might have hope.
ROMANS 15:4 NIV

*F*ather, what a treasure we have in Your Word. It's packed with life lessons about people who walked with You and knew You intimately. They experienced great success and tremendous failure. They were real people with real problems, people who struggled, just like we do, to grow in their faith. What an encouragement to press on, even as they did, to help others know You.

Always Prepared

Preach the Word; be prepared in season and out of season; correct, rebuke
and encourage — with great patience and careful instruction.
2 TIMOTHY 4:2 NIV

*L*ord Jesus, the courts say we are not free to preach Your Word in our schools. But our lives are living messages for others to see. When others do ask us about our faith, may we be ready to answer them. You have placed each of us believers in a particular place, at this particular time. May we be open to the opportunities You give us to speak wisely for You.

Daily Encouragement

But encourage one another daily, as long as it is called Today,
so that none of you may be hardened by sin's deceitfulness.
HEBREWS 3:13 NIV

*D*ear Lord, I know that encouragement isn't a one-time, one-size-fits-all gift. I need to give and receive it on a daily basis—at any time people find themselves in difficult, even hopeless situations, with hardened and discouraged hearts. May we help one another, keeping our eyes on You, staying focused on who You are and what You're doing in our lives. May we be true encouragers, Lord, in our daily walk.

The Power of Networking

*T*he key to business success or education is making connections. As educators, our job puts us in the center of the community. We are involved with families, helping our students navigate the school system. We are involved with other teachers, working together to make lifelong learning a reality for our students. We are involved with the community, seeking ways to learn from business and civic leaders, as well as educate them regarding what we are doing in our schools. The more we bring the community into our classrooms, the richer everyone will be—everyone wins when we work together.

One way to bring people into our classrooms is by having them volunteer. From moms who make cupcakes for holiday parties to senior citizens who help struggling students master basic skills in math and reading, volunteers make valuable contributions in our classes. Similarly, a wide variety of mentoring programs helps students by providing information and experience they need, along with guidance and direction.

Another aspect of community networking is prayer ministries. Groups such as Moms in Touch and See You at the Pole encourage small prayer groups to uphold the entire school in prayer. The heart of the Moms in Touch ministry is in groups of women who meet locally to pray for their schools or their districts. They let the teachers know of their presence and prayer support, often providing small tangible gifts to remind them of their care. See You at the Pole is a student ministry with a once-a-year event in September in which students gather at their local school's flagpole in the morning to pray for their school. Groups may meet more than that day, but their mission is to create a visible testimony of the power of prayer.

Both groups have a powerful impact on everyone: those who pray and those who are being prayed for. Lives are truly changed through these ministries and others like them, which bring the message of Jesus Christ to students.

Opportunities abound for us to bring the community into the classroom for educational purposes or to share our faith. In each case, we're helping to build relationships that the Lord can use for His purpose, and we're privileged to be a part of the process.

Seeking the Lord

Sow with a view to righteousness, reap in accordance with kindness;
break up your fallow ground, for it is time to seek the LORD
until He comes to rain righteousness on you.
HOSEA 10:12 NASB

O Lord, this word picture of farming is so helpful. In our communities, we are raising a special crop—planting seeds and caring for them as we raise the next generation. What an awesome responsibility You have placed in our hands! We desperately need Your wisdom as we sow, reap, and till the fallow ground, awaiting the rain of Your righteousness upon our crop.

Sowing in Peace

And the fruit of righteousness is sown in peace of them that make peace.
JAMES 3:18 KJV

*L*ord Jesus, we want to bear the fruit of righteousness in our schools and communities. Use us as peacemakers as we sow seeds of learning and seeds of faith. Our jobs are not always peaceful, but Your nature is full of peace; we trust that You can live through us as we deal with parents and others in the community. May everyone who passes through our doors sense the difference Your peace makes in our lives.

Reaping What We Sow

Do not be deceived: God cannot be mocked.
A man reaps what he sows.
GALATIANS 6:7 NIV

*D*ear Lord, we know this truth operates on several levels. Literally, what we plant is what comes up—in a garden or on a farm. Likewise, what we plant in the hearts and minds of our students will also yield a harvest. Furthermore, in our community, we will reap a profit according to our investment. May we invest in young people, in their education and character, and may You be glorified by the results.

Sowing and Reaping

Remember this: Whoever sows sparingly will also reap sparingly,
and whoever sows generously will also reap generously.
2 CORINTHIANS 9:6 NIV

*L*ord Jesus, make us generous sowers. We want to see an abundant harvest in our entire community. May our efforts to educate and evangelize reach beyond the doors of our classrooms. May we follow Your leading as we sow, planting and watering as You guide our hand. Forgive us for the times we sow sparingly. Increase our faith so we find ourselves confidently looking to You for an abundant harvest.

A Good Reward

From the fruit of his lips a man is filled with good
things as surely as the work of his hands rewards him.
PROVERBS 12:14 NIV

*D*ear Lord, we desire that our words and actions bear fruit—for Your glory, not our own. As we invest in our students, our schools, and our communities, may You be satisfied, even as we are filled with the pleasure of obeying You; may You be honored, even as we enjoy a reward for a job well done. Through it all, may many lives be changed as people meet You and believe in You.

Sure Reward

*The wicked man earns deceptive wages, but he
who sows righteousness reaps a sure reward.*
PROVERBS 11:18 NIV

Dear Lord, may our every effort be according to Your righteous character. As You lead us to work with those in our community, we desire that You, not we, be glorified. In each contact, each committee, and each project, may You be seen among us and may Your life make a difference. We want to be Your ambassadors in our schools and our communities, bringing many to know You.

Lending to the Lord

*One who is gracious to a poor man lends to the LORD,
and He will repay him for his good deed.*
PROVERBS 19:17 NASB

O Lord, may we see You in every need, knowing that our care for people demonstrates our care for You. Make us willing to give with grace from the abundance You have given us. Help us to surrender our tight grip on our time, our money, and our energy, knowing any sacrifice we make is small in comparison to the gift You gave: Your life for us.

Open Our Eyes

He who gives to the poor will never want,
but he who shuts his eyes will have many curses.

PROVERBS 28:27 NASB

*L*ord Jesus, keep our eyes open to the needs around us. Whether it's a student who needs shoes, a teacher who needs a break, or a parent who needs help learning to read, may we see and be involved in finding solutions. In our community, may we be willing to give whatever help You lead us to offer, knowing that You are the real supply for every lack.

Rejoicing and Bringing Sheaves

He who continually goes forth weeping, bearing seed for sowing, shall
doubtless come again with rejoicing, bringing his sheaves with him.

PSALMS 126:6 NKJV

*F*ather, our tears are never wasted as we labor in Your field. What a comfort, especially when we don't see results. Let us cling to Your promise of a harvest and faithfully plant seeds and water them, trusting You for an abundant crop. May we not be afraid of caring to the point of weeping for those we teach and those we work with—knowing our tears, like the seed, are not in vain.

Giving

"Give, and it will be given to you. They will pour into your lap a good measure—pressed down, shaken together, and running over. For by your standard of measure it will be measured to you in return."
LUKE 6:38 NASB

*L*ord Jesus, we just cannot out give You, no matter how hard we try. What a principle: The more we give, the more You give. May we be generous givers of our possessions and our faith. Not in order to have more, but because Your nature is expressed in our giving.

Loving the Alien

"So show your love for the alien, for you were aliens in the land of Egypt."
DEUTERONOMY 10:19 NASB

*F*ather, thank You for this reminder to care for those who are new to our area, perhaps even to our country. Help us sympathize with the challenges they face as they learn to get along in a new place, maybe even learning a new language. May they know Your love through our help. May we show them the same care we would want to receive if we were in a new place.

True Justice

*"Thus has the LORD of hosts said, 'Dispense true justice
and practice kindness and compassion each to his brother;
and do not oppress the widow or the orphan, the stranger or the poor;
and do not devise evil in your hearts against one another.'"*
ZECHARIAH 7:9–10 NASB

O Lord, help me have this view—to truly care for others. By nature, I am selfish and don't want to take the time or energy to reach out to anyone else. But Your love reaches out. I want to be a vessel You can use to touch others. Please make me a willing channel.

Honoring God

*He who oppresses the poor shows contempt for their Maker,
but whoever is kind to the needy honors God.*
PROVERBS 14:31 NIV

*F*ather, each person is valuable in Your sight as part of Your creation. From the lowliest to the greatest, every person is made in Your image. Don't let me lose sight of that truth. May Your love flow from me in kindness to others—whatever the need, whether information, encouragement, time, or money. Let me always find a way to help.

Many Counselors

Where there is no guidance the people fall,
but in abundance of counselors there is victory.
PROVERBS 11:14 NASB

*F*ather, You have dispensed Your gifts among us, and we can surely learn from one another, if we would only take the time to seek counsel. Forgive me for being independent and thinking I know more than I do. Thank You for putting me in positions where I have to ask others to help me. Together we can make a difference in our community, and it will be Your victory we celebrate together.

The Power of Struggle

*T*he United States emerged from intense conflict. How difficult it must have been for the Founding Fathers to break away from England and create a new republic.

Had you lived in the 1700s, would you have fought for independence? Would you have joined those laboring to create something new? Or would you have preferred to maintain ties with the mother country, hoping to keep the peace?

Teachers face similar questions today. In our schools, are we content to let others decide what's best for us and our students? Are we satisfied with the status quo or willing to fight for those things we believe will most benefit our students and society?

Tough questions, to be sure. But the practical issues are just as tough—how do we find time to influence local, state, and federal policies when we struggle to make lesson plans, grade papers, cook dinner, or keep up with the laundry?

Those Founding Fathers were fighters. They knew they needed to stand against England, but at times they experienced conflict among themselves. As they met for the Constitutional Convention that hot summer of 1787, tempers often flared. At one point, Benjamin Franklin stood to remind the men that they had once sought God's leading in prayer each morning before they began their work. Perhaps they should return to that practice, he suggested. "The longer I live," Franklin said, "the more convincing proofs I see of this truth—that God governs in the affairs of men. And if a sparrow cannot fall to the ground without his notice, is it probable that an empire can rise without his aid?"

The same power—prayer—that helped the Founding Fathers complete their work is available to us as teachers. We need it! Teachers today face tremendous pressure with the ever-increasing expectations of local, state, and federal rules—more paperwork, testing, social programs, and other responsibilities. Many of those demands threaten our traditional values, undermine the authority we represent, and question the very existence of God.

Sometimes it all seems to be more than we bargained for—after all, we only wanted to teach young people and help them become the best they can be. But let's remember the lessons of history and the power of prayer. Our struggle is not against flesh and blood but against principalities (not principals!) and powers (see Ephesians 6:12).

Let's struggle together on our knees.

Do Not Forget the Lord

Be careful that you do not forget the LORD,
who brought you out of Egypt, out of the land of slavery.
DEUTERONOMY 6:12 NIV

*D*ear Lord, in the United States today, we aren't that different from the children of Israel. We fought for our land as they fought to enter Canaan. Like them, we tend to forget our history, overlooking the God who led us to political and spiritual freedom. May we remember, Lord, what You brought us from and what You brought us to. May we never take our freedoms for granted but use them to proclaim Your truth.

Not Being Robbed

See to it that no one takes you captive through hollow and deceptive
philosophy, which depends on human tradition and the basic
principles of this world rather than on Christ.
COLOSSIANS 2:8 NIV

*L*ord Jesus, we are surely in a battle to remain faithful to You. Our hearts may long for You to be everything, but there are so many distractions! May we guard our hearts and minds against those thoughts and teachings that would pull us away from You. May we always keep our focus on Your Word, with Your people. Strengthen us to stand together, Lord.

Grace and Mercy

"But in your great mercy you did not put an end to them or abandon them, for you are a gracious and merciful God."

NEHEMIAH 9:31 NIV

*F*ather, You are so complex. On one hand, You are righteous, but on the other, You are gracious and merciful. Please have mercy on our country, Lord. Cause our people to turn back to You. Hold back the destruction that ungodly behavior deserves. May we as believers be bold to speak for You, helping others see You in all aspects of Your character. May many be led to repentance and salvation.

God Is in Control

"He changes times and seasons; he sets up kings and deposes them. He gives wisdom to the wise and knowledge to the discerning."

DANIEL 2:21 NIV

*L*ord God, You truly rule this earth. Nothing happens apart from Your will. Every leader is under Your control. May I always remember to pray for them—that all in authority would remember they are there by Your divine decree. Rule in our nation, Lord, as well as our schools and classrooms. Guide us by Your wisdom as we continually look to You.

Wisdom and Understanding

By wisdom a house is built, and by understanding it is established.
PROVERBS 24:3 NASB

Lord God, we need wisdom and understanding in our nation. Our country began with a stand for godly principles. May she continue to remain true to them so we don't lose what we've gained over the past two centuries. In my life and in my school, may I build according to Your truth, setting an example for my students to follow even after they leave my care.

Just Leaders and Laws

"By me kings reign and rulers make laws that are just."
PROVERBS 8:15 NIV

*L*ord, some days we wonder if our leaders and lawmakers know the meaning of "justice." So many selfish personal agendas creep into the laws of our land. We pray for You to give guidance to those in authority, leading them to make wise choices as they lead our country. In our schools, we ask for that same wisdom as we lead our students and govern our classes.

Building and Watching

Unless the LORD builds the house, its builders labor in vain.
Unless the LORD watches over the city, the watchmen stand guard in vain.
PSALM 127:1 NIV

*L*ord God, You are the builder and guardian of everything we do. From the smallest efforts in our classrooms, to local projects, to large national initiatives, we are dependent on You. May we always seek Your wisdom as we plan and build. In each step, Lord, let us trust You for guidance. May we never labor or stand guard in vain but unite with Your design and Your will.

Serve One Another

You, my brothers, were called to be free. But do not use your freedom to indulge the sinful nature; rather, serve one another in love.
GALATIANS 5:13 NIV

*L*ord Jesus, as You died for our spiritual freedom, many men (and women) have died for our political freedom throughout history. It's part of our national heritage—the willingness to lay down one's life for strongly held beliefs. May we never abuse the freedom bought for us but serve one another—putting the needs of others ahead of our own. May our teaching—and our citizenship—reflect Your sacrificial love.

Ready to Do Good

Remind the people to be subject to rulers and authorities, to be obedient, to be ready to do whatever is good.
TITUS 3:1 NIV

*L*ord, we need this reminder—we are by nature selfish, wanting to hold the reins of control. But every day we find ourselves in situations where we must heed school administrators or government leaders, whether or not we agree with them. We recognize that their authority is from You, Father. May our cooperation with the authorities be a strong testimony of Your Lordship in our lives.

Righteousness Establishes a Throne

It is an abomination for kings to commit wicked acts,
for a throne is established on righteousness.

PROVERBS 16:12 NASB

*F*ather, I appreciate the principle set forth here: There is a reward for those who act righteously and a punishment for those who act wickedly. In our classroom "kingdoms" where we rule and reign each day, may we be righteous leaders. We want to bring You blessing as we set an example of effective leadership for our students. May they see Your character in our actions and reactions as we lead.

Forgiveness and Healing

If my people, who are called by my name, will humble themselves
and pray and seek my face and turn from their wicked ways, then will
I hear from heaven and will forgive their sin and will heal their land.

2 CHRONICLES 7:14 NIV

*F*ather, our country surely needs a healing. We suffer from physical, emotional, social, and spiritual ills that only You can correct. Please touch the hearts of Your people, prompting them to pray, seek Your face, and turn from their wicked ways. We trust in Your promise that You will hear those prayers and bring forgiveness and healing.

Help from the Lord

My help comes from the LORD, who made heaven and earth.
PSALM 121:2 NASB

*T*hank You, Lord, for being our help. You, the Creator of heaven and earth, are always available to bring us aid. Nothing is too big or too small for Your attention. We can call on Your name, knowing that You hear us, whether we're concerned about our students, our schools, our personal lives, or the needs of our nation. At any moment of the day, You are available in prayer for worship, praise, or intercession. What an awesome God You are!

Turning to the Lord

Let the wicked forsake his way and the evil man his thoughts.
Let him turn to the LORD, and he will have mercy on him,
and to our God, for he will freely pardon.
ISAIAH 55:7 NIV

*L*ord, Your mercy is a precious gift. Like the Prodigal Son's father, You long for Your children to return, forsaking their wicked ways and evil thoughts. I'm thankful to have received Your pardon, Father. I want to share my faith with the people You've brought into my life—the teachers and students I encounter each day.

The House of the Righteous

*The wicked are overthrown and are no more,
but the house of the righteous will stand.*
PROVERBS 12:7 NASB

*D*ear Lord, Your judgment isn't something we always see immediately. Sometimes it seems wicked people get away with their awful behavior for a long time. But I know they aren't fooling You, Lord. In the end, it's the "house of the righteous" that stands. As I teach and care for my family, may I hold fast to Your eternal values, knowing they alone cannot be destroyed.

The Power of a Strong Foundation

So it was the devil, after all, who caused compulsory schooling," is Winifred Trask Lee's humorous, but historically based statement regarding education in America. Historians claim the "Olde Deluder Satan Acte" of 1647 was the beginning of what we know today as the American public school system. This act of the Massachusetts legislature begins, "It being one of the chief projects of that old deluder Satan to keep man from the knowledge of the Scriptures," then goes on to require each town to provide a school for its children.

The Puritans realized that education had taken a backseat to basic survival in the New World, and their youngsters didn't know how to read the Bible. So schools were established, each day beginning with the reading of the Bible. Other subjects followed.

For many years, schools were as varied as the teachers who ran them. In Massachusetts, Horace Mann pioneered the regulation of teacher training in the mid-nineteenth century. Those first steps paved the way for other educational reforms and improved standards.

At that time, prayer was still very much a part of America's social fabric. But over time, our nation—and our schools—moved away from dependence on God, culminating in the early 1960s' Supreme Court debates and decisions over the appropriateness of prayer in school.

In spite of all the changes in education, one thing remains the same: our desire, as teachers, to do our very best for our students. And it's through prayer that we can implement the greatest changes of all: the change in our own hearts and the hearts of our students.

Sure, there are plenty of difficult issues facing us. But President Jimmy Carter gave us wise advice when he quoted his grade school superintendent: "Adjust to changing times but cling to unchanging principles." If we do what we can and prayerfully leave the rest with our heavenly Father, He will make a difference in our classrooms.

Let's continue to pray as if it were 1647. Let's ask for God's guidance in our schools, for His presence to remain in our classrooms and His principles to affect our school systems. Let's remind ourselves that the power of prayer can help us overcome every challenge we face.

A Blessed Nation
Blessed is the nation whose God is the LORD.
PSALM 33:12 KJV

*F*ather, we want to see You bless our nation. But we know this promise is conditional. May we live up to those conditions, making You Lord of our lives—individually and corporately. Our Founding Fathers established our government on biblical principles; we long to see our leaders return to those principles, since their decisions affect what happens in our classrooms each day. May You have the preeminent place You deserve, Lord, in our hearts and in our nation.

The Righteous Stand Firm
When the storm has swept by, the wicked are gone,
but the righteous stand firm forever.
PROVERBS 10:25 NIV

*L*ord, may we anchor ourselves in You to survive the storms that inevitably come our way. In ourselves, we are weak, unable to withstand Satan's attacks. But with You as our righteousness, Father, we can stand firm in the battle. In the war for godly values, in the spiritual conflict for the souls of men, and in the daily battle to live as Christian witnesses, may we stand in You.

Enlarged and Extended

You have enlarged the nation, O Lord; you have enlarged the nation. You have gained glory for yourself; you have extended all the borders of the land.
ISAIAH 26:15 NIV

*F*ather, I believe You have blessed our nation because we have honored You. Remind us of our history—of Your intervention and Your blessing. You are the Source of our prosperity, both physical and spiritual. Because of You, we have the freedom to teach in our schools and to impact our students' lives for Your kingdom. Glorify Yourself through our efforts, Lord.

Exaltation or Disgrace

Righteousness exalts a nation, but sin is a disgrace to any people.
PROVERBS 14:34 NIV

*L*ord, clearly there are consequences to our actions, as individuals and as a nation. In our classrooms, we either reward or discipline our students for their behavior. May we always use Your Word as the basis of our rules, even if we can't teach the scripture directly. Grant us wisdom, Lord, in dealing with our students, as well as our society as a whole.

Builder of All

For every house is built by someone,
but the builder of all things is God.
HEBREWS 3:4 NASB

*D*ear Lord, we know that You are the Master Builder. You are the designer, the cornerstone, and the very material of the building. We desire to be one with You in Your work. May we never wander off to create monuments to ourselves. As we teach, may our lessons and our very lives reflect Your eternal design, turning the hearts of our students to You.

All Authority from God

Every person is to be in subjection to the governing authorities.
For there is no authority except from God, and those
which exist are established by God.
ROMANS 13:1 NASB

*F*ather, we agree to put ourselves under the authority You have established. Sometimes that's easy, when the ones leading us follow You. Other times it's not so simple—when our rulers don't share our godly values. But even then, Lord, may we accept that Your sovereign will is in effect, that You may be using those with whom we disagree to encourage us to pray for Your will.

The Blessing of Obedience

"See, I am setting before you today a blessing and a curse: the blessing,
if you listen to the commandments of the LORD your God, which I am
commanding you today; and the curse, if you do not listen."
DEUTERONOMY 11:26–28 NASB

*D*ear Lord, the results of our actions are real, though not always immediate: We can expect either a blessing or a curse. Your Word surrounds us, Father, woven into the fabric of our society—it's even on our government buildings and our money. Though some try to destroy that heritage, Lord, I want to remain true to You, following Your commandments and enjoying Your blessing as a reward.

Division Brings Ruin

*"Any kingdom divided against itself is laid waste;
and any city or house divided against itself will not stand."*
MATTHEW 12:25 NASB

Lord Jesus, oneness is a rare thing in our world. Nations fight each other, and people within nations fight among themselves over their differing opinions and beliefs. Even families and church congregations are divided, Lord. How contrary to Your character, Lord, and the deepest longings of our hearts. Something within us longs to connect with others. Help us as teachers to work in harmony, not demanding our own way. May we guide our students to work together, as well, so our classes are "kingdoms" not divided.

The Wise Man

"Therefore everyone who hears these words of Mine and acts on them, may be compared to a wise man who built his house on the rock. And the rain fell, and the floods came, and the winds blew and slammed against that house; and yet it did not fall, for it had been founded on the rock."
MATTHEW 7:24–25 NASB

Lord, we want to be wise, not foolish, builders—in our schools, in our homes, and in our churches. We want our work to be strong enough to withstand the troubles and storms that will come. May we build with eternal materials upon You, our Rock.

The Tent of the Upright
The house of the wicked will be destroyed,
but the tent of the upright will flourish.
PROVERBS 14:11 NASB

*F*ather, it seems that the wicked aren't suffering much destruction. Many of them actually appear quite prosperous. But that's according to my limited view of the world. Help me to fix my eyes on You, Father, leaving judgment in Your hands while I depend wholly on You to establish my "tent." May my teaching, my relationships, and my life all be upright. May I flourish as You make Your home within me.

Blessings Abound
A faithful man will abound with blessings, but he who
makes haste to be rich will not go unpunished.
PROVERBS 28:20 NASB

*F*ather, make us faithful. Not only to receive blessings, but to know and receive more of You. Keep us from the temptation of riches, and help us to trust in Your provision for our every need. May we always remember that Your blessings come not simply in a paycheck but often in the shy smiles and small accomplishments of our students.

Wise Building

*The wise woman builds her house, but with
her own hands the foolish one tears hers down.*
PROVERBS 14:1 NIV

Dear Lord, we want to be wise builders, trusting You for guidance each day. We don't want to tear down our work by foolish actions. As we teach, may we convey Your truth. As we deal with our students, may we care for them with Your love. As we fulfill the countless responsibilities our jobs require, may we enjoy Your peace amid the busyness. We want each aspect of our lives as teachers to reflect Your wisdom, resulting in a testimony that endures.

Precious Metals, Precious Stones

*Now if any man builds on the foundation with gold, silver, precious stones,
wood, hay, straw, each man's work will become evident; for. . .
the fire itself will test the quality of each man's work.*
1 CORINTHIANS 3:12–13 NASB

Lord Jesus, we want to use eternal materials as we build, as we invest in the lives of our students. May our words and deeds be gold, silver, and precious stones that last. Help us to put aside the wood, hay, and stubble, which will be destroyed. May our work be of Your highest quality, Father!

Built upon the Cornerstone

Now, therefore, you are no longer strangers and foreigners,
but fellow citizens with the saints and members of the household
of God, having been built on the foundation of the apostles and
prophets, Jesus Christ Himself being the chief cornerstone.
EPHESIANS 2:19–20 NKJV

*L*ord Jesus, we are blessed to be part of an eternal building of which You are the chief cornerstone. As we go about our daily tasks, remind us that what we see and touch on this earth is only temporary. Help us to arrange our priorities, knowing that our real home is with You.

My Family

The Power of Love

If as the African proverb says, it takes a village to raise a child, then it takes an entire family's complete support for a teacher to be able to do the job of an educator.

Teaching is not a nine-to-five job. In fact, many experienced teachers warn new staff about letting their career become consuming. In several polls, teachers express concern about being able to juggle teaching responsibilities with the rest of life.

Mornings in many teachers' homes may look like something out of the movie *Cheaper by the Dozen*, where lunches are put together in assembly-line fashion. Many find it easier to do those chores the night before. But evenings can be just as hectic.

One young man, whose mom worked long hours in adult education classes, asked one night, "Mom, will there be anything like dinner tonight?" instead of the usual question, "What's for dinner?" Most of us have our own survival secrets, whether it's bulk cooking, prepared ingredients, simpler meals, or eating out more often. The key is for each of us to find what works in our homes.

The most important key for surviving our busy schedules is to pray about every detail of each day. This may also become a family's most important support role. As moms or dads who teach, our families can lift up to God the needs that most stress us out and make life difficult for the family.

Knowing a loving family is behind us makes a huge difference in our being able to do our jobs. And having the family praying with and for us gives spiritual support, as well. The two together make for a winning combination.

The Greatest of These

But now faith, hope, love, abide these three; but the greatest of these is love.
1 CORINTHIANS 13:13 NASB

*L*ord Jesus, You showed love in Your living and in Your dying. You denied Yourself to obey the Father's plan. May we be channels of this love in our classrooms, in our homes, and in every area of our lives. Many have no idea what love is. They need to know the depths of Your selfless, sacrificing love which led You to the cross. Make Your unconditional love real to them through us.

Love One Another

"This is My commandment, that you love one another, just as I have loved you."
JOHN 15:12 NASB

*D*ear Lord, thank You for working in our hearts to make us even want to obey this commandment. Because of Your transforming work, we love others, not out of a sense of duty but out of the deep love within us, which spontaneously reaches out to touch others. You led the way, demonstrating Your love for us by laying down Your life. May it flow now through us, drawing many to seek and find You.

Heard by God

I love the LORD, because He hears my voice and my supplications.
Because He has inclined His ear to me, therefore I shall
call upon Him as long as I live.
PSALM 116:1–2 NASB

O Lord, how awesome to think that the God who created the universe listens to me—even leaning close to hear me. You hear my poured-out concerns and needs, along with my praise. Because I know I can trust You to listen, I will continue to call upon You and bring my every need to You.

That All Will Know

"By this all men will know that you are my disciples,
if you love one another."
JOHN 13:35 NIV

*L*ord Jesus, the loving relationships we have with other believers prove we are Your disciples. As I enjoy You with my family and have fellowship with other believing teachers, may we guard the oneness we have in You. May we always focus on the life we share by faith in You, not on any doctrinal differences. May the world see You in our love for one another.

He First Loved Us

We love, because He first loved us.
1 JOHN 4:19 NASB

*L*ord Jesus, thank You for loving us—enough to die for us. How can we not return such great love? And how can we not invite others to experience it with us? From our homes, where we love our families, and our classrooms, where we love our students, to the world in which we send them out to practice the lessons we have taught them—may You be glorified as others see and know Your love.

Love in Deed and Truth
My little children, let us not love in word or in tongue,
but in deed and in truth.
1 JOHN 3:18 NKJV

*F*ather, people surround us who need to see love in action. They've been told they are loved but haven't always seen actions to support those words. Keep us from adding to their hurt by saying we care then not showing it. Make our love genuine. May it be seen in the things we do, not only the things we say. May You be free to meet their true needs through us.

Love Is from God
Beloved, let us love one another, for love is from God;
and everyone who loves is born of God and knows God.
1 JOHN 4:7 NASB

*D*ear Lord, when we love You, it's so easy to love others! Your love is living, and it changes us. It fills us and overflows to those around us. So many in our world need to be loved: students whose homes are unstable or fellow teachers with difficult family situations. Even our own families need to be reminded of our love and Yours. Love through us today.

Owing Only Love

Owe nothing to anyone except to love one another;
for he who loves his neighbor has fulfilled the law.
ROMANS 13:8 NASB

Lord Jesus, out of Your great love, You paid our debt. As a result, we owe You our lives. Although we can never pay You back, we can show our love for You by loving others, following Your example. You have put people in our lives for us to love, showing them, perhaps for the first time, how great You are. May we be faithful to love our neighbor—whoever that may be today.

Overflowing Love

May the Lord make your love increase and overflow for
each other and for everyone else, just as ours does for you.
1 THESSALONIANS 3:12 NIV

Lord Jesus, our love increases and overflows as You fill us and flow out to others. Like a river, Your love is moving, causing us to love others in our families and other believers, as well. As we grow in love, we also have a greater capacity to love those who don't yet know You. We want to share You more and more—with everyone.

Abounding Love

And this is my prayer: that your love may abound
more and more in knowledge and depth of insight.
PHILIPPIANS 1:9 NIV

O Lord, what a tender relationship Paul had with these believers as he prayed for their love to abound and for them to really understand how to share that love. I desperately want to receive both more love and insight regarding how to show it. May I become close enough to my family and some at work that I can pray Paul's prayer for them. May Your love abound.

Brotherly Love

But concerning brotherly love you have no need that I should write to you,
for you yourselves are taught by God to love one another.
1 THESSALONIANS 4:9 NKJV

*F*ather, Your love has truly changed us. Even though we are teachers, we are also learners—being taught by You to love one another. What a joyous lesson! Yet sometimes it is difficult. Loving is not always easy; sometimes we need tough love. Teach us to depend upon You to know how to love people each day as their needs change.

Increasing Love

*We ought always to thank God for you, brothers, and rightly so,
because your faith is growing more and more, and the love
every one of you has for each other is increasing.*

2 THESSALONIANS 1:3 NIV

Dear Lord, what a precious relationship existed between Paul and the saints in Thessalonica. What confidence he had in their increasing faith and love. This is so normal, for Your life is a growing one. May we enjoy this level of trust—in our own families and our church families. Then together may we give thanks.

Sincere Love

*Now that you have purified yourselves by obeying the truth so that you
have sincere love for your brothers, love one another deeply, from the heart.*

1 PETER 1:22 NIV

Lord Jesus, Your transforming work in our hearts causes us to love others sincerely and deeply. Our students will know if our love for them is not real. Your love for us is the real thing; let us pass that on to them, especially to those who don't experience love at home. Thank You for giving us genuine love to share with others.

Loving Others

Beloved, if God so loved us, we also ought to love one another.
1 JOHN 4:11 NASB

O Lord, what a wonderful plan—the family, a safe place for us to learn about love and to practice loving. Children learn to love because they see their parents loving them. They automatically return that love to their parents and to their siblings. For those who haven't seen this example in their own homes, make our homes living testimonies of warmth and care. As Your family, joined by Your life, may we grow together in love.

The Power of Security

*W*e all remember Dorothy, clutching Toto, clicking her heels and saying, "There's no place like home; there's no place like home." Home is the place we hurry to at the end of the day. It's our own corner of the world where we are safe from the storms of life.

At least that's the way it's supposed to be. That's why, as a nation, we grieve together in times of natural disaster when we see people displaced by hurricanes, tornados, or floods. We weep over the loss of homes and lives. Many times we give financially or go in person help give food, shelter, and much needed comfort.

Why do we care? Because deep within us is the realization that we need a place to call home: a place where we are accepted and loved, a place where we can be comfortable and feel secure. God created us with both the desire to have a home and the feeling of incompleteness when it's missing. It's a picture of our relationship with Him— the reality of having a home in Him and the insecurity we feel until we are settled with Him.

The comfort and security we feel each day as we return home, the desire to create a warm atmosphere, the love we feel for our families and our joy in being with them is all a miniature of our real home with our Father and His family, the Body of Christ.

When the Prodigal Son came to his senses, he returned home to his father. Isn't it comforting to know we can return to our Father and be truly home? As teachers, we have the opportunity to share this truth with others. As we enjoy and share the shelter and security of our earthly dwellings, we can also share the reality of our eternal home.

We are sojourners, passing through our journey on earth. Just as Abraham spent his life looking for a city, we are seeking a permanent abode, an eternal dwelling place. When the Lord Jesus returns, we will be truly home—forever.

God, Our Rock

*"The LORD is my rock and my fortress and my deliverer; my God,
my rock, in whom I take refuge, my shield and the horn of my salvation,
my stronghold and my refuge; my savior, You save me from violence."*
2 SAMUEL 22:2–3 NASB

*D*ear Lord, You are so much to us—strength, protection, and salvation, to name only a few. We need Your strength to tackle the tasks before us, at work, in our communities, and in our homes. Life is exhausting—physically, mentally, emotionally, and spiritually. We need Your protection from all the difficulties, Lord. I thank You that we can rest in You, our Rock.

Our Redeemer

*But now, thus says the LORD, your Creator, O Jacob,
and He who formed you, O Israel, "Do not fear, for I have redeemed you;
I have called you by name; you are Mine!"*
ISAIAH 43:1 NASB

*F*ather, how wonderful to be called by You—to be called by name. You created and redeemed me, showing Your great love for me. Many of my students don't believe anyone cares about them. Help me let them know of Your love for them, Lord. May I show that same love in my home, my church, and all of my other relationships.

Under His Wings

*He shall cover you with His feathers, and under His wings you
shall take refuge; His truth shall be your shield and buckler.*
PSALM 91:4 NKJV

*F*ather, what a comfort to know we're securely sheltered
under You. Like a mother hen, You supply us with everything we need. Likewise, You can provide for those
we work with—students and staff alike. We rest in Your
truth, which surrounds us and offers safety in the storms
of life. Like armor, Your Word protects us in battle.

Our Dwelling Place

Lord, You have been our dwelling place in all generations.
PSALM 90:1 NASB

O Lord, the homes we live in are just pictures of our true
home in You. We are protected from the elements, with a
roof over our heads and walls surrounding us. We are safe
from those who could harm us. We are comfortable in
the midst of all that is dear and familiar. Yet some never
know this kind of warmth on earth. Nor do they know
anything of an eternal dwelling. May our homes and
classrooms demonstrate Your love and lasting security.

God with Us

And I heard a loud voice from the throne saying, "Now the dwelling of God is with men, and he will live with them. They will be his people, and God himself will be with them and be their God."
REVELATION 21:3 NIV

*F*ather, how amazing to realize that You desire to be one with us. You desire to live with us and be our God. You created us for this very purpose. Not each of us individually but together. May we give ourselves to this today in our homes and schools as a foretaste of our eternal home.

Our Refuge

*Trust in him at all times, O people; pour out
your hearts to him, for God is our refuge.*
PSALM 62:8 NIV

*D*ear Lord, thank You for being so available—we can
talk to You anytime. We can pour out all our concerns
about our teaching, our students, our fellow staff members, our families—everything. There is no problem too
small or too big for You. We are safe in You. May others
be drawn to the security they sense in us and be led to
trust You with every detail of their lives.

Dwelling in Safety

*I long to dwell in your tent forever and
take refuge in the shelter of your wings.*
PSALM 61:4 NIV

*F*ather, we desire to dwell with You, to know Your presence within us and in fellowship with other believers. We
want to share this with all who seek such a true home.
Give us opportunities to offer the permanence of Your
home to others and the courage to speak when doors
open to us. Even in our temporary, earthly homes, we are
thankful for Your protection.

Trusting in God

Those who know your name will trust in you, for you,
Lord, have never forsaken those who seek you.

PSALM 9:10 NIV

*D*ear Lord, how blessed we are to know Your name. What riches are in Your name: enough to meet the needs of the students I teach each day, the staff I work with, and the members of my own family. We can trust in Your name and in Your promise that You never forsake those who seek You. People may walk away from us, but we can always count on You.

Our Defender

But let all those rejoice who put their trust in You;
let them ever shout for joy, because You defend them;
let those also who love Your name be joyful in You.

PSALM 5:11 NKJV

*F*ather, how we need joy! And we have it as we rest in You. May we shout joyfully, letting others hear of our glorious defender. In a world full of danger and fear, we have One who loves us and provides for us. We love You and rejoice in the many ways You care for us. You defend us against every negative force, leaving us securely trusting in You.

Peace and Safety

I will lie down and sleep in peace, for you alone,
O Lord, make me dwell in safety.

PSALM 4:8 NIV

*F*ather, we know how hard it is to rest when we don't feel safe and secure. In You, we have real rest. This doesn't mean there will never be problems or even danger. We face them every day. Yet it means we don't have to worry or fear. We are safe in You. For many, home is not a safe place. May they find rest and peace in Your arms.

Reward and Refuge

"May the Lord repay you for what you have done.
May you be richly rewarded by the Lord, the God of Israel,
under whose wings you have come to take refuge."

RUTH 2:12 NIV

O Lord, thank You for the tender story of Ruth, showing us our place in You. You are the best lover, even rewarding our faith by giving us a safe place to dwell, just as Boaz cherished Ruth. Thank You for each one You have brought to us to care for, to love and shelter, leading them to You.

Righteous Homes

The LORD's curse is on the house of the wicked,
but he blesses the home of the righteous.
PROVERBS 3:33 NIV

*D*ear Lord, we want our homes to be places You can use to draw others to Yourself. Of course we want Your blessing—not for the sake of the blessing alone, but so Your presence may fill our homes. We need to experience You in a real way, alone and with our families, so we are equipped to face our jobs at school. As we seek You, may we find Your abundant supply of love.

A Lasting City

For here we do not have a lasting city,
but we are seeking the city which is to come.
HEBREWS 13:14 NASB

*L*ord Jesus, like You, we are merely passing through this earth. We do not belong here. Our real home is an eternal city in which we dwell with You forever. All the things we love and treasure about our lives here are just shadows of our real life, our real treasure, and our real home. May we know and share You as our true dwelling place and our true security.

The Dwelling of God

So then you are no longer strangers and aliens, but you are fellow citizens with the saints, and are of God's household. . .in whom you also are being built together into a dwelling of God in the Spirit.
EPHESIANS 2:19, 22 NASB

*D*ear Lord, this is our true destiny, being built together by Your Spirit into a place where You can live. Thank You that we belong to Your family! Open a way for us to bring many more in, especially those who have never experienced a loving family in their homes.

My Health

The Power of Prevention

We probably know enough about being healthy to fill a textbook. The challenge, of course, is putting what we know into practice. With a to-do list longer than our attendance roster, who has time to exercise and watch every calorie? But can we afford *not* to take care of the body God has given us?

This is one area where Benjamin Franklin's maxim "An ounce of prevention is worth a pound of cure" is good advice. When we change our own health habits, we benefit—and we help our students recognize the importance of taking care of themselves, too. We can begin with the acronym SEE. It stands for *S*leep, *E*xercise, and *E*at well.

Be sure to get enough rest each night. Though it's tempting to stay up late to finish one more project or to get up early for a jump start on the day's activities, guard your sleep. You'll begin each new day more rested and alert.

Next, find an exercise plan that works for you. It doesn't have to be expensive or elaborate—it just has to work. Think of things you're already doing and turn them into exercise. For example, since you have to go to the grocery store anyway, park at the far end of the lot and rack up some extra walking time on the way in and out of the store. As you unload your groceries, try a few knee bends or toe touches. At school, bring your students into the fun—do stretches, deep breathing exercises, even more vigorous activities as a group. Plan movement into your day, especially when the weather is bad and everyone is stuck inside. Maybe you could create a contest between classrooms or even schools in the community. In Dyersville, Iowa, residents lost nearly a ton of weight when almost four hundred people joined in a ten-week weight loss program.

Finally, eat healthy meals in reasonable amounts. Consider your allotted calories for the day like budgeted money. You only have so much to spend each day, so make wise choices.

Just as caring for our bodies can prevent illness, caring for our spirits brings many benefits. Another acronym to remember is ACTS. In prayer, we come to God in *A*doration, worshipping Him for who He is. Then we *C*onfess our weaknesses and sins. That's followed by *T*hanksgiving, receiving forgiveness and wholeness. Finally we bring our requests to Him in *S*upplication.

Good habits can keep us healthy—inside and out. We don't want sickness—physical or spiritual—to keep us from the students we care so much about!

Physical and Spiritual Exercise

For physical training is of some value, but godliness has value for all things, holding promise for both the present life and the life to come.

1 TIMOTHY 4:8 NIV

Dear Lord, help me find balance in my life, as I care for both the physical and eternal things. I need to care for the body you've given me, without losing sight of what really matters—the development of godly habits and character. Please help me care for my physical body through healthy eating, exercise, and rest. And show me how to strengthen my spiritual self through Bible reading, prayer, and fellowship.

The Fear of the Lord

The fear of the LORD adds length to life, but the years of the wicked are cut short.

PROVERBS 10:27 NIV

Father, teach me what it means to fear You. Not that I cower and hide, because You are love. But I know there are aspects of Your character that should bring a healthy fear to my heart: You're a jealous God; You want to have first place in my heart. May I serve You through my teaching, reflecting Your love, and helping others to make You Lord of their lives.

Our Inheritance

*"You shall write them on the doorposts of your house and on your gates,
so that your days and the days of your sons may be multiplied on
the land which the LORD swore to your fathers to give them,
as long as the heavens remain above the earth."*
DEUTERONOMY 11:20–21 NASB

O Lord, may we be like the children of Israel, surrounded by Your Word and Your presence, experiencing Your blessing from one generation to the next. While I can't physically write Your Word on the doorposts of my classroom, I pray that I might live it out in my every word and deed today.

We Are But Grass

*All flesh is grass, and all its loveliness is like the flower of the field.
The grass withers, the flower fades, when the breath of the LORD
blows upon it; surely the people are grass. The grass withers,
the flower fades, but the word of our God stands forever.*
ISAIAH 40:6–8 NASB

*F*ather, our earthly life is so temporary. But Your Word is forever. When I'm focused on my difficulties—thinking they will last forever—help me to remember how fleeting these trials are. Remind me that I'll live forever with You!

A Time for Everything

There is an appointed time for everything.
And there is a time for every event under heaven.
ECCLESIASTES 3:1 NASB

*F*ather, what a beautiful passage. There is such balance in the pairs listed: A time for birth and death, tears and laughter, love and hate. What rest it brings me, trusting in You for each event, each season of this life. May I see Your design in my life each day, accepting each appointed time and reveling in Your master plan. May my teaching reflect this faith and joy.

Bought with a Price

Do you not know that your body is a temple of the Holy Spirit, who is in you, whom you have received from God? You are not your own; you were bought at a price. Therefore honor God with your body.
1 CORINTHIANS 6:19–20 NIV

*D*ear Lord, what an amazing truth—You actually live in me! You paid the ultimate price to redeem me, so I yield all I am to You. May I be an acceptable dwelling place for Your Spirit, Lord. May You flow freely through me in all I do today, helping others to recognize Your claim on their lives.

The Way to Prosperity

Humility and the fear of the LORD bring wealth and honor and life.
PROVERBS 22:4 NIV

*L*ord Jesus, I want to please You with a proper attitude, humbling myself before You and having a healthy respect for who You are. May my heart reflect this, not for what it brings me, but for what it brings You. May others see Your faithfulness as You bless me, Lord. May my "wealth and honor" come from the relationships You bring me, as I invest my time and energy in those around me.

Instruments of Righteousness

*Do not let sin reign in your mortal body. . . . And do not
present your members as instruments of unrighteousness to sin,
but present yourselves to God as being alive from the dead,
and your members as instruments of righteousness to God.*
ROMANS 6:12–13 NKJV

*L*ord Jesus, I ask You to reign in me today, in my thoughts, words, actions—and body. In practical matters, Lord—like what I eat and how I treat my body—may I yield to You. Please take control over each part of my body, and make my life a testimony of Your Lordship.

An Imperishable Prize

*Everyone who competes in the games exercises self-control in all things.
They then do it to receive a perishable wreath, but we an imperishable.*
1 CORINTHIANS 9:25 NASB

*L*ord, life is like a game. We're all competing for a prize— and for me, as a believer, the goal is eternal. Help me today to focus on how I compete. May I discipline myself so I can continue the race set before me. It's hard, Lord, with so much on my plate. But I bring every decision to You, asking for self-control as I manage my daily life.

Competing by the Rules

*Also if anyone competes as an athlete, he does not
win the prize unless he competes according to the rules.*
2 TIMOTHY 2:5 NASB

*L*ord Jesus, You modeled this kind of a life for us. You always followed the will of Your Father, doing nothing apart from Him. May I follow You in such complete harmony. As a soldier trained for battle or an athlete trained to compete, may I live my life as an educator according to the rules of Your kingdom. I want to be sure of winning the prize, Lord!

Remembering Godly Instruction

*My son, do not forget my teaching, but keep my commands in your heart,
for they will prolong your life many years and bring you prosperity.*
PROVERBS 3:1–2 NIV

*L*ord, may I focus on remembering Your Word—more than dreaming of long life or prosperity. No matter how many days You give me, may they be filled with knowing and following You. However much money You give me, may my heart be filled with the riches of Your Word. And may this true wealth flow through me, bringing spiritual health and prosperity to my students and coworkers.

Walk Carefully

*Therefore be careful how you walk, not as unwise men but as wise,
making the most of your time, because the days are evil.*
EPHESIANS 5:15–16 NASB

*D*ear Lord, teach me to make the most of my time. When I am up to my neck in papers to grade, lessons to plan, home and family to care for, keep me mindful of my true priorities. Teach me how to best use each minute, how best to care for each person You've placed in my life.

Don't Worry

"Who of you by worrying can add a single hour to his life?"
MATTHEW 6:27 NIV

*L*ord, how easy it is to worry. There are so many things I can be concerned about, but please help me bring them to You in prayer. Lord, I don't want to hug them to myself as if they were some cherished treasure. My worrying not only won't add time to my life, but it could actually shorten it. May I care for myself by giving my cares to You.

Wise Advice

*Listen, my son, accept what I say, and
the years of your life will be many.*
PROVERBS 4:10 NIV

*F*ather, I thank You for the wisdom You give us. What a blessing! And what a promise—long life. May I use my days wisely, Lord, learning from You, then living those lessons out in my home and school. You are the best teacher of all, Father. May I learn from Your example to teach with wisdom and understanding.

My Joys

The Power of Gladness

*O*ne of the greatest joys in the life of a teacher is when a student "gets it." I like to call that "the aha moment." But that's not the only joy we as teachers experience. Joy is an integral part of the Christian life.

Jesus told several parables that reflected joy: The joy of the shepherd when he finds his lost sheep. . .the joy of the woman when she finds her lost coin. . .the joy of the father when his lost son returns to him. Dad was so happy he threw a party!

Pollyanna is one of the great characters of fiction. She stars in a series of fourteen books in which she faithfully plays her "glad game" and teaches it to others around her. The idea is simple, but it's actually a tremendous spiritual exercise requiring great faith and an intimate knowledge of God as a loving Father.

When we first meet Pollyanna, she's telling the maid about the "glad game" she had played with her father. "The game was to just find something about everything to be glad about—no matter what 'twas. The harder 'tis, the more fun 'tis to get 'em out. Only—sometimes it's almost too hard—like when your father goes to heaven, and there isn't anybody but a Ladies' Aid left."

Later she explains to the minister how her father created the game. "He wouldn't *stay* a minister a minute if 'twasn't for the rejoicing texts—all those that begin 'Be glad in the Lord' or 'Rejoice greatly' or 'Shout for joy.' Once, when father felt specially bad, he counted 'em. There were eight hundred! He said if God took the trouble to tell us eight hundred times to be glad and rejoice, He must want us to do it. Why, it was those texts, too, father said, that made *him* think of the game—about finding something in everything to be glad about."

Whatever the exact number of verses, the principle of joy is clearly found throughout scripture. In 1 Thessalonians 5:18 (NIV), for example, the apostle Paul says, "Give thanks in all circumstances, for this is God's will for you in Christ Jesus." Our hearts are changed by thankfulness, and we are able to experience true joy.

As teachers, let's play Pollyanna's "glad game" ourselves, looking for things to be thankful for no matter what might be going on in our lives or classrooms. Let's live in such an attitude of gratitude and help others do the same. As Pollyanna's friend Jimmy says, "It would revolutionize the world if everybody would really play it."

It would, indeed. May the revolution begin today, in us.

Rejoicing in the Lord

Rejoice in the Lord always; again I will say, rejoice!
PHILIPPIANS 4:4 NASB

Dear Lord, how it fills my heart to rejoice in You. For who You are, for all that You do, for what You mean to me. And thank You for repeating the command. For reminding me, because I forget so quickly when things get hard. Repetition is a good teaching method, and surely You are the best teacher. Today in my classroom, may I rejoice in You. No matter what happens around me, within my heart, I can rejoice!

Remembering His Benefits

Bless the LORD, O my soul, and forget not all his benefits.
PSALM 103:2 KJV

Lord Jesus, as I remember all of Your benefits, I cannot help but praise You and bless Your name. My home, my health, my job, my students: such abundant riches! Truly I have much to be thankful for. I recognize that it all comes from Your hand. May I never forget how graciously You have blessed me and how far Your benefits extend—in this life unto eternity!

Finding the Lost

"And when he finds it, he joyfully puts it on his shoulders and goes home. Then he calls his friends and neighbors together and says, 'Rejoice with me; I have found my lost sheep.'"
LUKE 15:5-6 NIV

*D*ear Father, what joy You feel when something lost is found! May we be so eager to celebrate when our students make new discoveries. When a student successfully fights to learn a new concept, to overcome an obstacle, to reach a goal, may we call one another with such news and rejoice together in the growth of our students.

Rejoicing in God's Love

I will be glad and rejoice in Your mercy, for You have considered my trouble; You have known my soul in adversities.
PSALM 31:7 NKJV

*D*ear Lord Jesus, thank You that we can be real with You. When problems are overwhelming and we feel unable to face another day as a teacher, we can tell You all about it. Whether it's a challenging student, a difficult coworker, or just an accumulation of too much work in too little time, in Your love and mercy, we can find comfort, joy, and strength to face another day.

God Rejoices over Us!

As a young man marries a maiden, so will your sons marry you; as a bridegroom rejoices over his bride, so will your God rejoice over you.
ISAIAH 62:5 NIV

*W*ow, Lord, You rejoice over us! Forgive me for being surprised that You experience such feelings in Your desire for Your people to be established as Your own. How awesome, that my joy is merely a shadow of Yours. For we are the object of Your love, Your Bride—come quickly, Lord Jesus!

Our Refuge

Let the righteous rejoice in the LORD and take refuge in him;
let all the upright in heart praise him!
PSALM 64:10 NIV

O Lord, sometimes we just need to escape. In the midst of a hectic day, we can hide in You. You are a safe place to which we can always run, even when we cannot leave our classrooms. In our hearts, we can reach out to You and find exactly what we need to see us through. Thank You for being such a refuge.

Rejoice and Be Glad

This is the day the LORD has made; let us rejoice and be glad in it.
PSALM 118:24 NIV

*L*ord Jesus, it is wonderful to know You made this day. It is Your design. How amazing that You know everything that will happen, when I am at home and when I am at school. I know I can trust You—that You will be with me through each moment of the day—today and tomorrow and the next day. Whatever comes my way, I can rest in You, rejoicing in each situation and rejoicing in You.

Bringing Cheer

An anxious heart weighs a man down, but a kind word cheers him up.
PROVERBS 12:25 NIV

*D*ear Lord, may I bring cheer to others through my speaking today. So many around me are anxious and weighed down by heavy loads. My coworkers are burdened by problems with students and at home. Just keeping up with our schedules can be difficult. Yet many have other serious concerns that make the load even harder to bear. Let words of real encouragement flow from my mouth today, bringing joy to others and making their loads just a bit lighter.

Be Glad in His Salvation

In that day they will say, "Surely this is our God;
we trusted in him, and he saved us. This is the LORD,
we trusted in him; let us rejoice and be glad in his salvation."
ISAIAH 25:9 NIV

*F*ather, I want to have this kind of testimony at my school: that others would know You are a part of my life, that I trust in You, and that you bring salvation. That those around me would even be able to trust You for themselves because they see evidence of Your faithfulness in my life. That many would rejoice through Your life in me.

Joyful in Hope

Be joyful in hope, patient in affliction, faithful in prayer.
ROMANS 12:12 NIV

*L*ord Jesus, as I consider the hope I have in You, my heart is joyful. In You, I can be patient when things are difficult. With such a joyful expectation, I can pray, believing You will answer. I long to be a living testimony of joy and patience in my school. I yearn to be a teacher who prays faithfully for the needs of each student, not giving up until the prayer is clearly answered. Make me such a teacher.

Rejoice, Pray, Give Thanks

*Rejoice always; pray without ceasing; in everything give thanks;
for this is God's will for you in Christ Jesus.*
1 THESSALONIANS 5:16–18 NASB

*L*ord Jesus, how wonderful it is that joy, thanksgiving, and prayer are so intertwined. When we continually spend time with You in prayer, we become spontaneously joyful and grateful. We don't have to remain on our knees—we couldn't do that with our busy schedules—but our hearts can remain in intimate fellowship with You. Our students will benefit from our prayerful communion. What joy to be in Your will!

Giving Thanks

Always giving thanks to God the Father for everything,
in the name of our Lord Jesus Christ.
EPHESIANS 5:20 NIV

*D*ear Father, this verse reminds me to accept everything that comes into my life as from You. The challenging student, the difficult lesson, the impossible schedule—it's all from Your hand, and I can give thanks accordingly. I cannot control many situations in my day, but I can control my reactions by having a grateful heart and praying in Your precious name. Truly this brings joy and gladness to my heart.

I Will Rejoice

Although the fig tree shall not blossom, neither shall fruit be in the vines;
the labour of the olive shall fail, and the fields shall yield no meat; the flock
shall be cut off from the fold, and there shall be no herd in the stalls: yet I
will rejoice in the LORD, I will joy in the God of my salvation.
HABAKKUK 3:17–18 KJV

*L*ord Jesus, when there is nothing outwardly to be thankful for, we can still rejoice in You. When we lack what we need for, our classes, when we can only see hardship and failure, You are still our salvation.

A Joyful and Glad Heart

He sent the people to their homes, joyful and glad in heart
for the good things the LORD had done for David and
Solomon and for his people Israel.
2 CHRONICLES 7:10 NIV

*D*ear Lord, I want to have a joyful and glad heart. I want to recognize the good things You have done in the past as well as the good things You are doing right now. When I go home at the end of the day, I want to review these good things and see that I have much to rejoice over!

The Power of Contentment

*P*eace and contentment are elusive qualities that always seem out of reach. A little bit more, we think, then we will have arrived. More money, more stuff, and more success. Yet often the opposite is true—our real need is to have less: less to do, less responsibility, and fewer possessions. Then we might be in a position to have more of what really matters—time to do the things we love, time for people we love, and time for God.

Dan was a teacher whose family struggled for years to manage on his salary. When his daughter wanted her own new car, he felt bad that he couldn't provide one for her. Yet what he gave her ended up being much more valuable. He helped her find a used car and taught her how to take care of it. She later admitted that the mechanical know-how she picked up was something none of her friends had. In addition, she had learned to live within her means. Even more important, dad and daughter spent time together along the way. When his daughter drove off in her first new car, after finishing college and landing a job, Dan was no longer ashamed of his inability to provide. God had provided what they'd both needed.

In our schools, budget cuts often make it difficult to have all the supplies we would like. But as teachers, we are among the best at making do with what we have, whether it's a room that is too small, too dark, too hot, or too cold; books that are old or falling apart; or a lack of materials to work with.

Contentment is a choice we make, often on a daily basis, as we decide how to react to challenges. Whatever the situation, we can bemoan our lot, find creative alternatives for dealing with the situation, or accept what we have and make the best of it. And of course, we can pray, which helps both our attitude and our need. As God's children, we can choose to be content because we know our Father and our eyes are on Him. Then we'll experience the peace we were looking for all the while.

Our Daily Bread

Give us today our daily bread.
MATTHEW 6:11 NIV

*D*ear Lord, enough for today is all we ask. Enough food, enough money, enough of everything we need—our daily bread. Not our weekly allotment but what we need today. In our profession, we also ask for enough—enough patience to deal with our classes, enough energy to do what the day requires, enough love to meet the needs of our students. Enough of You. Thank You, Lord. You are always enough for what is before us.

Content with What We Have

Make sure that your character is free from the love of money,
being content with what you have; for He Himself has said,
"I will never desert you, nor will I ever forsake you."
HEBREWS 13:5 NASB

*L*ord Jesus, help me learn contentment. It's interesting that this reference to being content is followed by Your promise to be with us. Perhaps the two are more closely related than we think. Concern about the future and worries about money can't exist if we truly believe You are with us and caring for us.

Godliness with Contentment

But godliness with contentment is great gain. For we brought
nothing into the world, and we can take nothing out of it.
But if we have food and clothing, we will be content with that.
1 TIMOTHY 6:6–8 NIV

O Lord, forgive me for gathering things, thinking they will make me happy. Remind me what is truly valuable—gaining You. We can't take our possessions with us when we die, yet we can take Your life into eternity. Let's teach with this view of what is important.

Content in Any State

Not that I speak from want, for I have learned to be content in whatever circumstances I am. I know how to get along with humble means, and I also know how to live in prosperity; in any and every circumstance I have learned the secret of being filled and going hungry, both of having abundance and suffering need.
PHILIPPIANS 4:11–12 NASB

*F*ather, I confess, I have not learned this secret. Yet I desire to know this kind of contentment. In good times and bad, help me learn to accept what comes as from Your hand.

God Is on Our Side

The Lord is on my side; I will not fear: what can man do unto me?
PSALM 118:6 KJV

*L*ord Jesus, You promise to be on my side, whatever the battle. Whether it is a fight within myself, a disagreement with someone else, or even a struggle with You, You stand at the Father's right hand, interceding on my behalf. What more could I want? What greater assurance could I require? Forgive me for doubting the outcome of the battle. May I remain as faithful to You as You are to me.

Where Your Treasure Is

"Do not store up for yourselves treasures on earth,
where moth and rust destroy, and where thieves break in and steal.
But store up for yourselves treasures in heaven, where neither moth
nor rust destroys, and where thieves do not break in or steal;
for where your treasure is, there your heart will be also."
MATTHEW 6:19–21 NASB

*L*ord Jesus, as teachers, we have daily opportunities to lay up treasure in heaven by investing truth in our students. This is the best investment we can make—keep us mindful of the treasure You value.

We Can't Take It with Us

Do not be overawed when a man grows rich, when the splendor
of his house increases; for he will take nothing with him when he dies,
his splendor will not descend with him.
PSALM 49:16–17 NIV

*F*ather, deliver us from the "keeping up with the Joneses" attitude, even in our profession. When others prosper, let us not be envious. When others have the best students, let us trust that we have those we need, those who need us. When friends speak of wealth, remind us of the eternal riches that are ours. And let us be thankful.

Prayer for Our Portion

*Keep deception and lies far from me, give me neither poverty nor riches;
feed me with the food that is my portion, that I not be full and deny
You and say, "Who is the LORD?" or that I not be in want and steal,
and profane the name of my God.*

PROVERBS 30:8–9 NASB

*D*ear Lord, make this our daily prayer so we can learn
contentment: that we never have so much we forget You
nor so little we curse You. Our salaries may not be the
biggest, but You supply exactly what we need.

Rest and Safety

*I will lie down and sleep in peace, for you alone, O LORD,
make me dwell in safety.*

PSALM 4:8 NIV

*F*ather, in You is true contentment, true rest, and safety.
With You, we have no worries, no fears. Whatever the situation
is at work, we can trust that You are in control. May
we share this peace with coworkers who fret and worry
about their lives. They may be facing financial problems,
marital difficulties, or problems with their students. Let us
pray for them and encourage them. And may our peaceful
attitude be a testimony of Your faithfulness.

Perfect Peace

"You will keep him in perfect peace, whose mind
is stayed on You, because he trusts in You."
ISAIAH 26:3 NKJV

*L*ord Jesus, thank You for this marvelous promise! In few areas of our lives, can we reach perfection, yet that is what You offer. When we are focused on You, there is peace. When there is no peace, remind us that our minds have wandered away from You. Through Your Word and through other believers, we can stay focused on You even amid stressful days and difficult situations. What a testimony in a world so lacking in peace!

He Is with Us

"And lo, I am with you always, even to the end of the age."
MATTHEW 28:20 NASB

*D*ear Lord, what comfort and peace to know You are with us forever. There are so few things we can rely on, so few people we can trust completely. You are completely available to meet every situation, and we rest both in the promise and in the reality of Your presence. Whether we are following our plans or a detour, we can choose to be content because You are with us. That is all we need.

Naked We Came, Naked We Depart

Naked a man comes from his mother's womb,
and as he comes, so he departs. He takes nothing
from his labor that he can carry in his hand.
ECCLESIASTES 5:15 NIV

*F*ather, it is sobering to realize that after all our working and striving to attain our goals in this life, we will leave it just as we came—with nothing. Keep this ever before us so that we aren't distracted by temporary gain. May we model a simple lifestyle and eternal values through the choices we make regarding our time and possessions.

The Power of Praise

*F*ear is a normal part of life. Sometimes it protects us, making us act carefully around ice or fire. But at other times, our fears take on a life of their own, causing us unreasonable stress and anxiety.

New seasons of life bring their own fears. For us as teachers, there was college and certification. Then there was that incredibly stressful first year of teaching. In time, we settled into a routine, but even then various crises probably arose, at school or at home, threatening to destroy the calm we'd enjoyed. Questions of job security, funding levels, and ever-increasing requirements can nibble away at our peace.

But as believers, we can take steps to combat much of the fear in our lives by remembering that we have a loving heavenly Father. When we face real problems—and everyone does—we have a powerful Friend who gives us an eternal perspective on each and every situation. God will see us through whatever may happen.

The very best antidote to fear is the Bible, which contains the remedy for every worry we have. We can encourage one another with the Word when problems and fears arise then pray together over each concern.

We can even turn the scriptures into song. As the psalmist said, "Our God inhabits the praise of his people." When we lift our voices in praise, our fears lose their hold on our hearts. Our focus turns once again to the Lord Himself, and we are empowered to face our frightening situations.

Let's go forth, like David, facing our giants and fighting our fears in the strength of the Lord! He always gives us victory.

A Steadfast Heart

My heart is steadfast, O God, my heart is steadfast;
I will sing, yes, I will sing praises!
PSALM 57:7 NASB

Lord, when my heart is set on You, everything is fine—
even when life is a mess outwardly. And this teaching job
can be messy. There's the physical mess of the room and
all the paper, the emotional messes students face in their
homes, and the spiritual messes of those who don't know
You. Sometimes, Lord, when I look around me, fear rises
up. But when I look to You, my racing heart calms. Fear
vanishes, and I can sing Your praise.

Trusting God

Whenever I am afraid, I will trust in You.
PSALM 56:3 NKJV

Dear Lord, some days fear is my constant companion. But
I thank You for coming alongside me and chasing away
every doubt. I can look to You, over and over, throughout
the day, and fears dissolve. I'm human, Father, so those uncertainties never completely go away. But I know that You
will always give me victory over worry, whether I'm considering my students, my finances, or my health. Thank
You, Lord, for always being available to me.

Whom Shall We Fear?

The LORD is my light and my salvation; whom shall I fear?
The LORD is the strength of my life; of whom shall I be afraid?
PSALM 27:1 KJV

*L*ord Jesus, You are so much to me! You provide for my every need. When I'm afraid, please help me remember Your love and care for me. In You, Lord, I'm strong enough to face the most difficult class, the most overwhelming schedule, the most frightening situation. Nothing that I fear, Lord, is bigger than You. You can meet the challenge and overcome it.

My Strength and Song

"The LORD is my strength and my song; he has become my salvation.
He is my God, and I will praise him, my father's God, and I will exalt him."
EXODUS 15:2 NIV

*D*ear Lord, I want to be like the children of Israel, singing praise for Your salvation. All too often, my eyes are on the pursuing enemy, not on You. But when I look at You rather than the challenges I face in my classroom, I am strengthened. I am saved from my fear—and You give me a victorious song to sing.

Singing Praises

I will tell of Your name to my brethren;
in the midst of the assembly I will praise You.
PSALM 22:22 NASB

*L*ord Jesus, I want to be a living testimony, sharing my faith with those I encounter each day. As I interact with other teachers, may my words be full of praise to You—for all You do and all You *are*. May I be quick to tell of answered prayer, sharing how you've helped me deal with a difficult student or how you've met a specific need I brought to you. I want You to be glorified in my school!

A Joyful Heart

The LORD is my strength and my shield; my heart trusts in him, and I am
helped. My heart leaps for joy and I will give thanks to him in song.
PSALM 28:7 NIV

*L*ord, so many things trouble me. But those fears melt in Your presence. When my patience reaches its end, You see me through. When the work is overwhelming, You energize me to face it. Thank You for the strong promises in Your Word. As I meditate on them, I see more clearly that You are with me to provide whatever help I need.

Garment of Praise

And provide for those who grieve in Zion—to bestow on them a
crown of beauty instead of ashes, the oil of gladness instead of
mourning, and a garment of praise instead of a spirit of despair.
ISAIAH 61:3 NIV

*L*ord, we need to change clothes—to trade in our despair for garments of praise. You can make that happen as You fill us, transforming our sadness to joy, our fears to praise. We can bring all our worries and fears to You; then we can experience Your peace and joy.

Continuous Praise
I will bless the LORD at all times:
his praise shall continually be in my mouth.
PSALM 34:1 KJV

*F*ather, Your constant love and provision should spur me to unending praise. But I don't always see You in my circumstances, so I don't always praise You as I should. Help me remember that You are worthy of praise, even when things aren't going well. Instead of complaining about my students and administration, I want to be a testimony to others by blessing and praising You. May my lips speak forth praise all day.

A New Song
He put a new song in my mouth, a song of praise to our God;
many will see and fear and will trust in the LORD.
PSALM 40:3 NASB

*F*ather, I thank You for the new song You've put in my heart. Please add new verses to that song as I continue to grow in You. Nearly every day, Lord, brings a new awareness of how great You are. You see me through the difficulties and give me wisdom to handle classroom situations I could never manage alone. May others see Your work in my life and believe for themselves.

Our Helper

So we may boldly say: "The LORD is my helper;
I will not fear. What can man do to me?"
HEBREWS 13:6 NKJV

*L*ord Jesus, I'm not always bold. But I can boldly stand on the truth that You are my helper and I don't need to be afraid. Many things frighten me, but I can trust that You will help me face each one. I know that I can't be everything my students need. I can't guarantee their success or mine. Those truths will never change. But You change me, Lord, and I am not afraid.

Our Value

"So don't be afraid; you are worth more than many sparrows."
MATTHEW 10:31 NIV

*F*ather, if You notice all those little birds, You surely know about my life. You're aware of all my concerns, my weaknesses, my insecurities, and my failures. You know the limits of my patience and endurance. You know the things that are hard for me. You know every detail of my life—at school, at home, and inside my heart. So I don't need to be afraid. Since You already know my life, You'll provide all that I need.

Sons, Not Slaves

For you did not receive a spirit that makes you a slave again to fear, but you received the Spirit of sonship. And by him we cry, "Abba, Father."
ROMANS 8:15 NIV

*F*ather, You know that fear enslaves us all at one time or another. Sometimes it's hard just to get up for the day. We face problems at school, difficulties in the lives of our students, our own family concerns—sometimes it's more than we can handle. Thank You that as sons (and daughters!), we can rest in Your love and care. We can leave our fears with You, Lord.

A Spirit of Power

For God has not given us a spirit of fear, but of power and of love and of a sound mind.
2 TIMOTHY 1:7 NKJV

*L*ord Jesus, fear doesn't come from You. I know that in my heart; sometimes I forget, though, because fears can be so powerful. But when I turn to You, something happens inside me. I'm strengthened, able to see things more clearly and able to love. We all need those qualities in our interactions at school, Lord. Please give me and my colleagues Your power, Your love, and Your mind.

Perfect Love

There is no fear in love; but perfect love casts out fear, because fear involves torment. But he who fears has not been made perfect in love.
1 JOHN 4:18 NKJV

*D*ear Lord, my love is so imperfect, and there's nothing I can do to make it better. Some days I can barely be polite to people, much less loving. I know that's so far short of the way You want me to deal with people, Lord. Fill me with Your love so it flows through me and touches the people You have put in my life. May Your perfect love replace my limited love, Father.

My Leisure

The Power of Recharging

*A*re you laughing, just seeing the title of this chapter? *Leisure!* you may think. *What's that? I can't get to everything I need to do, much less have time left over. And if I did have free time. . .*

Think about a battery charger. It forces power into a still object, equipping it to perform its job. Our cell phones, for example, won't work if we don't occasionally turn them off and plug them into the charger. Nobody considers the phone a failure—it has simply run out of power. After some time on the charger, it will be useful again. In the same way, none of us scold our cars for running out of gas, telling them that if they would just try harder, they could manage another few miles. No, we simply fill up the gas tank.

As teachers, we don't like to think of ourselves as having limits. But we're among the most likely to experience burnout because our work is people oriented and we are dedicated to our profession. The high standard we set for ourselves—the very thing that makes us good at what we do—can also be our downfall.

God established the principle of rest: After six days of creation, He rested. He pictured this in the Old Testament law of the weekly Sabbath and in fields which were to lie fallow every seven years. In the New Testament, Jesus often went off alone to pray. Likewise, He took the disciples away for teaching.

It's important for us all to recharge by taking on something new, something we've always thought we'd enjoy doing and can be passionate about, not just another task to complete. We need to invest in recreation that completes us, something we *must* do. What helps one person relax might exhaust another, so each of us must be sure to find our own key to restoration, not somebody else's. And we must be willing to change occasionally if the hobby becomes a chore.

So let's be bold and put time for ourselves on our schedules. Time for physical rest, emotional restoration, and spiritual recharging. Let's stop looking at these things as occasional rewards and view them instead as investments—the very things that recharge our energy and enable us to keep going, at home, in the community, and in the classroom.

The Seventh Day

"Six days you shall labor, but on the seventh day you shall rest;
even during the plowing season and harvest you must rest."
EXODUS 34:21 NIV

*F*ather, You set the pattern of working for six days then rest. In biblical law, we also see this enforced, even during busy seasons. Forgive us for not taking time to recharge, especially when we're busy. Help us find the proper balance of work and rest so we can approach our jobs each day fresh and ready to face our students with our best.

Restoring Our Souls

He makes me to lie down in green pastures;
He leads me beside the still waters. He restores my soul.
PSALM 23:2–3 NKJV

O Lord, how we need the refreshment of lying in green pastures and walking by still waters—literally and figuratively. We need the physical restoration nature brings, as well as the spiritual revival a time of quiet rest offers. As we work, we get weary, and our souls need to be restored so we have the emotional and spiritual strength to carry on. Refresh us today as we rest in You.

Reviving Our Souls

The law of the LORD is perfect, reviving the soul.
PSALM 19:7 NIV

*D*ear Lord, we come to You in Your Word, and we are revived, given new life. This is so refreshing. Help us make this part of our schedule—meeting You in Your Word each day. Just as we rest each night for our bodies' health, we need spiritual rest, as well. We are empowered as we touch You in Your Word. Daily refreshed, we can fulfill the many responsibilities required of us as teachers.

Our Rock

From the ends of the earth I call to you, I call as my heart grows faint;
lead me to the rock that is higher than I.
PSALM 61:2 NIV

*F*ather, You are indeed a strong rock for us to depend on. When the burdens of the day weigh heavy on our hearts and we feel we can't go on, we can call out to You, knowing You hear us, knowing You will help us. No matter where we go, we can reach You in prayer, calling out to You, even when we feel faint. Thank You for being so available.

Waiting on the Lord

He gives strength to the weary, and to him who lacks might
He increases power. . . . Yet those who wait for the LORD will gain
new strength; they will mount up with wings like eagles, they will
run and not get tired, they will walk and not become weary.

ISAIAH 40:29, 31 NASB

*D*ear Lord, thank You that these verses don't say strength is given only to those who try harder or to those who have it all together. You help the weak and the weary as we rest in You and wait upon You.

Renewing the Inner Man

Therefore we do not lose heart, but though our outer man is decaying,
yet our inner man is being renewed day by day.

2 CORINTHIANS 4:16 NASB

*L*ord Jesus, how grateful we are for the contrast between the outer man and the inner man, the temporary and the eternal. You are renewing us each day as we contact You through the Bible and in prayer. How we need this supply to equip us to work with our students. May they see the effect of our true renewal as we grow in life.

Repentance and Rest

"In repentance and rest you will be saved,
in quietness and trust is your strength."
ISAIAH 30:15 NASB

*D*ear Lord, we are truly renewed in You. When everything is clear between us, we are free to trust You and therein find strength. Keep us in line with Your design for our lives: resting in You, using our energy to accomplish Your will, and following You each day as we teach. Even as we pursue hobbies and other interests, may we remember our real renewal is in Your life and the faith You have put in our hearts.

Be Still and Know

Be still, and know that I am God; I will be exalted
among the nations, I will be exalted in the earth!
PSALM 46:10 NKJV

*F*ather, I need help even in finding a way to be still. There is always so much going on around me. The to-do list is always longer than I could ever complete. Yet I know I need to just turn aside from all the tasks at hand and enjoy a quiet moment with You. How can I hope to hear Your still, small voice if I never slow down and remain quiet?

Fly Away and Rest

I said, "Oh, that I had the wings of a dove!
I would fly away and be at rest."
PSALM 55:6 NIV

O Lord, how often I have wanted to escape! No more papers to grade, no more lessons to plan, no more meetings to attend, no more students in need of discipline. It sounds wonderful! Yet in reality, in the midst of the duties that clamor for my attention, the only true escape is to You. What a blessing to know You in the quiet of my heart, even when outwardly situations are chaotic.

Come Away with Me

*Then, because so many people were coming and going that they
did not even have a chance to eat, he said to them, "Come with
me by yourselves to a quiet place and get some rest."*
MARK 6:31 NIV

*L*ord Jesus, what a special invitation—to come away
with You to a quiet place for rest. You know what it's
like to have crowds pressing in on You. You know how
they ask questions. You were a teacher, too—with a difficult class. Therefore, I know You understand my need
for peace and quiet.

Rest for Our Souls

*"Come to Me, all who are weary and heavy-laden, and I will give you rest.
Take My yoke upon you and learn from Me, for I am gentle and
humble in heart, and you will find rest for your souls.
For My yoke is easy and My burden is light."*
MATTHEW 11:28–30 NASB

*L*ord Jesus, some days are exhausting. You understand
both my physical and spiritual weariness, and You provide
rest for each of them. When I am joined to You, the load
is easier to bear because You help carry it and because You
are with me.

On the Mountain Alone

After he had dismissed them, he went up on a mountainside
by himself to pray. When evening came, he was there alone.
MATTHEW 14:23 NIV

*D*ear Lord, how good to see that You went off by Yourself to be alone to pray. Sometimes we need to do this, too. Maybe we've been extra busy and need a break, or we have a problem requiring time to think and pray through, or we need wisdom to deal with a student or situation in our class. Whatever the need, it's good to go away, alone, and pray. Thank You for this example.

A Time for Everything

To everything there is a season, a time for every purpose under heaven.
ECCLESIASTES 3:1 NKJV

*D*ear Lord, just as there are seasons to be busy, there are surely seasons to be quiet and rest. We need balance to survive our jobs as teachers. Sometimes we give and give, then collapse because we haven't allowed any time to rejuvenate ourselves. Remind us that rest is an investment so we can keep going, not a sign of weakness. Help us stabilize our days with time for work and time for rest.

Praying All Night

*It was at this time that He went off to the mountain to pray,
and He spent the whole night in prayer to God.*
LUKE 6:12 NASB

*L*ord Jesus, if You spent the night in prayer, how much more we need to spend time seeking the Father's will, especially when our workload is heavy. In those times, we need Your wisdom and direction; You never fail to provide that when we come to You in prayer. Thank You for being so available! May we bring our every need before You, with the full assurance that You hear and answer.

The Power of Purpose

*G*oal setting is important because it helps us see the connection between "someday" and today, what we want to accomplish in class and at home. Without specific goals, we are like a person in a car, revving the engine, spinning the wheels, but going nowhere. Without deadlines and a plan, we'll never accomplish as much as we'd like to. Have we taken time to identify our goals and list the steps we need to take to reach them?

As believers, we accomplish all of this under an umbrella of prayer, considering what God desires for us to do and how He will enable us to achieve the plans we make.

Do we still have plenty of dreams left on the back burner? Or once our career goals are pretty well met, do we just settle in and enjoy the ride for twenty or thirty years? We're likely to get stale if we don't continue to set new goals that stretch our mental and spiritual muscles.

Every few months, it's good to review written goals and check our progress. We may need to revise some of the steps, as life interferes and demands flexibility. Since few of us will live long enough to complete all the plans we can think up, we also need to prioritize our lists and focus on the most important goals God has for us. Then we can eliminate things not directly related to our goals, streamlining our lives. As a result, we'll become better stewards of the gifts the Lord has given us. Our lives will be more focused, and we'll be more in tune with the Lord regarding how we spend our time and energy.

Let's seek God's guidance as we set goals and establish a plan of action. Each of our lists will be different, but together we create a beautiful tapestry as we each follow our individual purpose in God's master plan.

God's Purpose

And we know that all things work together for good to those who love God,
to those who are the called according to His purpose.

ROMANS 8:28 NKJV

*D*ear Lord, what security to know You and Your purpose. This doesn't mean everything goes our way but that You are using everything for our good, which is to be conformed to Your image. Good days, bad days; success, failure; coordination, frustration: It's all working together for good. Thank You that we can know You in every situation of our lives.

Successful Plans

Without consultation, plans are frustrated,
but with many counselors they succeed.

PROVERBS 15:22 NASB

*F*ather, it's so easy to be isolated and make decisions on our own. It takes time to seek advice. We forget what wisdom our friends, families, and coworkers can offer us, if we'd only ask. As we think of our next steps, whether personal or professional, remind us to seek guidance from You and from those You've placed in our lives. Then we will succeed, and we can rejoice together in what we accomplish.

A Holy Calling

*Who has saved us and called us with a holy calling, not according
to our works, but according to His own purpose and grace which
was given to us in Christ Jesus before time began.*
2 TIMOTHY 1:9 NKJV

*L*ord Jesus, we are called to so much more than our profession. We are called to fulfill Your purpose, an even
higher calling than that of teaching. We want to cooperate with all You are doing in us and in those around us.
Thank You that this eternal calling is by Your grace, not
our effort.

In His Steps

*For you have been called for this purpose, since Christ also suffered for
you, leaving you an example for you to follow in His steps.*
1 PETER 2:21 NASB

O Lord, what a privilege to follow You, even when it
includes suffering. Our walking in Your steps today is
not merely something outward, an imitation of Your life.
Rather it is Your life within us, carrying out Your words
and actions on the earth today. With our students, families, friends, and other believers, we are called to live out
Your life, wherever that leads.

Our High Calling

I press toward the mark for the prize of
the high calling of God in Christ Jesus.
PHILIPPIANS 3:14 KJV

*D*ear Lord, thank You for this heavenly calling. We are pursuing something higher than any earthly goal. All our attainments in this life pale in comparison to knowing You, possessing You, and being possessed by You. As we strive to accomplish the personal and professional goals we set for ourselves, let us never lose sight of our real goal and calling, which is higher and longer lasting.

Running the Race

Therefore we also, since we are surrounded by so great a cloud of witnesses,
let us lay aside every weight, and the sin which so easily ensnares us,
and let us run with endurance the race that is set before us, looking
unto Jesus, the author and finisher of our faith, who for the joy that
was set before Him endured the cross, despising the shame, and has sat
down at the right hand of the throne of God.
HEBREWS 12:1–2 NKJV

*L*ord Jesus, we want to live as You lived on earth—with one purpose driving us in all we do.

Deep Waters

The purposes of a man's heart are deep waters,
but a man of understanding draws them out.
PROVERBS 20:5 NIV

O Lord, we are so complicated, yet how inspiring that You plumb the depths within us. As we consider our goals, our beliefs, and our purposes in life, may we experience the fulfillment of Your promise that You will be found by those who truly seek You. Keep us from remaining shallow and missing the joy of a deeper life. Help us simplify our lives and schedules so we have time to pursue You.

Gaining Christ

*I count all things to be loss in view of the surpassing value of knowing
Christ Jesus my Lord, for whom I have suffered the loss of all things,
and count them but rubbish so that I may gain Christ.*

PHILIPPIANS 3:8 NASB

Dear Lord, we strive to gain so much that is meaningless in light of eternity. Keep us focused on You, the truly valuable One. Whatever it costs to follow You, we want to be willing to pay the price to know You more, to have You fill our lives.

To Live Is Christ

For to me, to live is Christ and to die is gain.

PHILIPPIANS 1:21 NIV

Lord Jesus, I confess, I'm not always able to say this with Paul, but I would like to be. I desire this kind of consecration. Have Your way in my heart—wean me from all the things of this earth that draw me away from You. Often they're good things, but they're not You. As You fill me, may others see Your life in me. May You be magnified in me.

True Profit and Gain

*"For what will it profit a man if he gains
the whole world, and loses his own soul?"*

MARK 8:36 NKJV

*D*ear Lord, remind us of what our lives are for—to gain You, not wealth, possessions, and fame. The degrees, awards, and successes we achieve are nothing if we don't have You and You don't have Your way in our lives. May we live before our students in such a way that our values and priorities testify to an eternal standard, not an earthly one.

A Minister and Witness

*"But get up and stand on your feet; for this purpose I have appeared to you,
to appoint you a minister and a witness not only to the things which you
have seen, but also to the things in which I will appear to you."*

ACTS 26:16 NASB

*L*ord Jesus, may we live as though Paul's calling were our own. May we have a clear view of why we stand before our students each day. Yes, we have information to share with them, but even more, we have truth to minister according to what we have seen and heard. This is our true calling.

Plans of the Heart

In his heart a man plans his course, but the LORD determines his steps.
PROVERBS 16:9 NIV

*D*ear Lord, may we learn to wait upon You for guidance as we make plans for our lives. We want our hearts to match Yours. In the big things and the small things, as well, we don't want to rush forward without consulting You. In our profession, our family, and our personal interests, we want our plans to reflect oneness and a coordination with Your heart's desire so that You may be glorified.

A Wise Heart

Teach us to number our days aright, that we may gain a heart of wisdom.
PSALM 90:12 NIV

*F*ather, we don't know how long our lives will be. Help us to plan wisely yet always with eternity in view. We could have many more years to live or merely days on this earth. Help us make each day count for eternity—with the awareness that this could be our final opportunity to speak for You, even as we hope for many more years to be Your witnesses. May we have Your view of time.

He Holds Our Hands

*The steps of a man are established by the LORD, and He delights
in his way. When he falls, he will not be hurled headlong,
because the LORD is the One who holds his hand.*
PSALM 37:23–24 NASB

*F*ather, what comfort to know You hold our hands. You
don't promise that we'll never fall but that You will never
let go. May we share this assurance with our students.
Just as we are with them in class when they try new
things, You remain with them—forever.

The Power of Hope

*T*he future. For many of us, that includes many more years in the classroom. For some, with retirement drawing near, those days are fewer in number.

Wherever we stand on the career spectrum, we all have plans for the future. But often, things happen to change even the most carefully laid plans. Hundreds of challenging scenarios involving everything from needs in our families to a change in our own health can arise to interfere with the course we have charted for ourselves.

No matter how trying such changes can be, we as Christians can find peace in the storm. We can turn to the Lord in prayer, both for the planning of our lives and the rearranging of those plans when detours occur.

The artist Thomas Kincaid tells of a former English teacher who retired, not knowing what he would do with the rest of his life. He turned his love of books into a new hobby, learning to bind and repair old volumes. The avocation grew into a fund-raising project for a local hospice, filling his hours with meaningful work and supplying much-needed funds for the charity.

Whether we have many teaching years before us or are on the cusp of retirement, all human beings need meaningful work and human interactions. And we need hope—both for this life and the next. God created us to keep looking to Him, trusting in His promises. Whatever our situation, we develop and maintain hope through prayer, communing with our heavenly Father, resting in His arms, trusting Him in whatever comes our way.

With all the uncertainty in our lives and the lives of those we teach, there is One we can count on. Yesterday, today, and tomorrow, God remains constant, faithful, and true.

"Although the world is full of suffering," Helen Keller once said, "it is full also of the overcoming of it." That is true hope—continual overcoming, until our ultimate hope of eternity with the Lord becomes reality.

Hoping for What We Do Not See

For in hope we have been saved, but hope that is seen is not hope;
for who hopes for what he already sees? But if we hope for what we
do not see, with perseverance we wait eagerly for it.

ROMANS 8:24–25 NASB

*L*ord Jesus, these verses capture the essence of hope: assurance, certainty, and expectation. As we face the future, with all the uncertainties of daily living, we know we can trust You. We can believe Your promises and live peacefully in the hope that You are fulfilling them.

The Hope of His Calling

I pray that the eyes of your heart may be enlightened,
so that you will know what is the hope of His calling, what
are the riches of the glory of His inheritance in the saints.

EPHESIANS 1:18 NASB

*L*ord, may the apostle Paul's prayer for the believers in Ephesus extend to us today—and through us to those whose lives we influence. We experience such riches in Christ. What a marvelous calling that guides our lives! Shine in our hearts today, Lord, so that we may see our hope and glorious inheritance even more clearly.

Hopeless without God

At that time you were without Christ. . .
having no hope and without God in the world.
EPHESIANS 2:12 NKJV

*F*ather, there was a day when I was hopeless, without You in this world. How desolate a hopeless life is! Today many around me—faculty and staff in my building and students in my classes—are living in despair. May I share my faith boldly, Lord, offering the hope I possess, since I have been brought near to You through Christ.

New Heaven, New Earth

Then I saw a new heaven and a new earth; for the first heaven
and the first earth passed away, and there is no longer any sea.
And I saw the holy city, new Jerusalem, coming down out of heaven
from God, made ready as a bride adorned for her husband.
REVELATION 21:1–2 NASB

*D*ear Jesus, how we want to be part of Your bride, prepared and adorned for You, our husband. May we live worthy of being Your bride, awaiting You as the consummation of our hope. With the Spirit, we cry, "Amen. Come, Lord Jesus!"

Christ, the Hope of Glory

To whom God would make known what is the riches of the glory of this mystery among the Gentiles; which is Christ in you, the hope of glory.

COLOSSIANS 1:27 KJV

*L*ord, it's delightful to know a secret! We are those to whom You have unveiled the mystery of the ages—Christ in us, our hope of glory. How rich we are to have You living within us, expressing Your life as we go through our daily tasks. May that life be evident in our classrooms today!

Fixing Our Hope on God

Instruct those who are rich in this present world not to be conceited or to fix their hope on the uncertainty of riches, but on God, who richly supplies us with all things to enjoy.

1 TIMOTHY 6:17 NASB

*D*ear Lord, compared to most of the world, we in the western world are wealthy. May we never boast or trust in our riches, since they don't last. Instead, may we focus on what we have experienced of Your rich supply within us—an eternal treasure. And may we share the wealth in our schools!

Overflowing Hope

*May the God of hope fill you with all joy and peace as you trust in him,
so that you may overflow with hope by the power of the Holy Spirit.*
ROMANS 15:13 NIV

*L*ord, may we be like sponges—absorbing hope then dripping and spreading it over everyone we touch! As we trust You and our hope increases, may it affect every single person we encounter, whether we're running errands, preparing meals for our family, teaching our classes, or whatever. Empower us to be channels of hope, Lord.

Our Blessed Hope

For the grace of God has appeared, bringing salvation to all men,
instructing us to deny ungodliness and worldly desires and to live sensibly,
righteously and godly in the present age, looking for the blessed hope and
the appearing of the glory of our great God and Savior, Christ Jesus.
TITUS 2:11–13 NASB

*L*ord Jesus, may I live expectantly with the hope of Your appearing ever before me. I know, with that truth in view, I would live my days differently, even teach my class differently. May Your grace fill my instruction, and may I reflect that eternal viewpoint.

Holding on to Hope

Let us hold unswervingly to the hope we profess,
for he who promised is faithful.
HEBREWS 10:23 NIV

*L*ord Jesus, I can only hold on to hope because of Your faithfulness. Yet so many things cause me to doubt You: personal setbacks, changes of plans, even disruptive students. Life in general can be hard. Sometimes my grip on hope is tight, but sometimes I barely hold on at all. Yet You remain faithful, true to Your promises. May I cling to You in every situation I face today.

Desire Fulfilled

*Hope deferred makes the heart sick, but when
the desire comes, it is a tree of life.*

PROVERBS 13:12 NKJV

*L*ord, every person knows the heartache of having a cherished dream dashed to pieces. Because we have all experienced disappointment, our hope in You can be a true comfort. We see evidence of Your faithfulness each day as You transform hearts and work miracles in us, reminding us of Your continual loving presence.

A Reason for Our Hope

*But in your hearts set apart Christ as Lord.
Always be prepared to give an answer to everyone who
asks you to give the reason for the hope that you have.*

1 PETER 3:15 NIV

*J*esus, I want You to be my Lord—not only in word but in reality. I want to have an answer for those who ask about the hope I have. Not some rehearsed speech, but a response that truly meets the needs of their hearts. Whether I'm talking to a fellow staff member, a parent, or a student, may my words make a difference.

Great Is His Faithfulness
This I recall to my mind, therefore I have hope. The LORD's lovingkindnesses indeed never cease, for His compassions never fail. They are new every morning; great is Your faithfulness. "The LORD is my portion," says my soul, "Therefore I have hope in Him."
LAMENTATIONS 3:21–24 NASB

*F*ather, when I consider who You are, how can I not trust You? You are faithful, compassionate, and loving. Fill my thoughts today not with lesson plans or facts from textbooks but with remembrances of all You are and all You have done. As I interact with others, may my words reflect these marvelous truths.

A Living Hope
Blessed be the God and Father of our Lord Jesus Christ, who according to His great mercy has caused us to be born again to a living hope through the resurrection of Jesus Christ from the dead.
1 PETER 1:3 NASB

*L*ord Jesus, Your resurrection brought us a *living* hope— not something fake or dead but really and truly alive! No matter how difficult my circumstances or how frustrated I become with classroom situations, I can praise You. Your resurrection life conquered death and can now overcome every challenge I face. May I share this great salvation with those around me!

God, Our Hope

"And now, Lord, what do I wait for? My hope is in You."
PSALM 39:7 NKJV

*F*ather, patience has never been easy for me. Yet when I look to the future, all I can do is trust You to care for every detail. I give You my finances, my health, my job, and my family. I thank You that I can trust You to care for each and every aspect of my life. And when I leave this earth, my real life with You will continue throughout eternity. This is my true hope, Lord.

The Power of Investment

*E*ach of us hopes to make a difference in the lives of students. If we didn't, we probably wouldn't submit ourselves to the rigors of the educational system, especially in the public venue.

At the end of the movie *Mr. Holland's Opus*, the band director is humbled when a roomful of former students gather in his honor. One proclaims, "We are your symphony. We are the music and the notes. We are your opus." Few of us will have such things said publicly about our career, yet the comments are probably true. We are each producing our magnum opus through our teaching. But we don't do it for man's applause. We serve in faith, knowing we teach because it's where God has put us, and we do it for Him.

We may never enjoy this Hollywood version of teaching, yet we know teachers do make a difference. Many of us are in the field of education because a teacher touched our lives. Let's watch for divine appointments. Then let's be willing to invest in the young people we encounter, knowing God brought them into our lives.

Our legacy is multifaceted: who we are and what God has put into us influence our teaching, along with the information we impart to our classes. As Christians, we not only impart information; we are ambassadors on earth representing a heavenly kingdom. Many are searching for the hope and joy we have in Jesus; let us be cheerful givers of this Person within us.

Each of us hopes to sow moral seeds, which will produce good character; educational seeds, which will result in a love of learning; and eternal seeds, leading to faith and eternal life. Sometimes we're not sure the seeds have taken root—but we keep planting and watering and praying that the Lord will bless our efforts for His glory.

Follow Me

Now you followed my teaching, conduct,
purpose, faith, patience, love, perseverance.
2 TIMOTHY 3:10 NASB

*L*ord Jesus, I want to live in such a way that my actions, even my character, can be closely scrutinized and found acceptable as a pattern. For Your glory, not my own, I live before other people on a day-to-day basis. I never want to be the cause of someone stumbling or turning away from You. Shine through me so they see You when they look at me, for You are the best teacher, the only one truly worthy of being emulated.

Faithful Men

And the things that you have heard from me among many witnesses,
commit these to faithful men who will be able to teach others also.
2 TIMOTHY 2:2 NKJV

*L*ord Jesus, each of us desires to have faithful men to whom we can commit our faith. Whether they are students, friends, coworkers, or family members, give us each some to teach, to be built together with. We have classes full of students to whom we teach reading, writing, and arithmetic. Beyond this, our hearts' desire is to dispense Your life into others. Let us be teachers of both earthly and heavenly matters.

Crown of Righteousness

I have fought the good fight, I have finished the race, I have kept the faith.
Now there is in store for me the crown of righteousness, which the Lord,
the righteous Judge, will award to me on that day—and not only to me,
but also to all who have longed for his appearing.
2 TIMOTHY 4:7–8 NIV

*L*ord Jesus, I want to be able to say these things at the end of my life. Help me order my life in such a way that if it ended today, I would be confident that I have lived faithfully.

Wisdom and Understanding

Blessed is the man who finds wisdom, the man who gains understanding,
for she is more profitable than silver and yields better returns than gold.
PROVERBS 3:13–14 NIV

*F*ather, I want to invest my life in true riches. I want to leave a legacy of eternal value. When people remember me, may it be for the wise words You spoke through me, for the character qualities You worked into me, and for the love You poured out to them. As students reflect on my class, may they recall the welcome they received and the atmosphere they enjoyed, more than the facts they learned.

How to Boast

*"Let not a wise man boast of his wisdom, and let not the mighty
man boast of his might, let not a rich man boast of his riches;
but let him who boasts boast of this, that he understands and knows Me,
that I am the Lord who exercises lovingkindness, justice
and righteousness on earth; for I delight in these things."*
JEREMIAH 9:23–24 NASB

O Lord, may this be our boast—that we understand
and know You. Surely this is the best investment we can
make. For it delights You and brings joy to our hearts, as
well.

A Wise and Mighty God

*"You are great in counsel and mighty in work, for your eyes are open
to all the ways of the sons of men, to give everyone according to
his ways and according to the fruit of his doings."*
JEREMIAH 32:19 NKJV

*D*ear Lord, we can never hide from You. You know our
every word and action, even our motives. One day there
will be a total reckoning, and we will receive a reward
based on how we lived. May our actions today reflect
this as we plant seeds that produce a harvest pleasing to
You.

God Is Not Mocked

*Do not be deceived, God is not mocked; for whatever
a man sows, this he will also reap.*

GALATIANS 6:7 NASB

*F*ather, we see justice defined in Your character. In the end, each of us will be paid according to our investments. May we sow seeds of eternal value as we teach our classes and interact with students as well as staff. Keep us from depending upon our own reasoning so that our sowing is of You, not of ourselves. May we be sober before You, regarding our responsibility as sowers of truth.

Imitating and Inheriting

*We do not want you to become lazy, but to imitate those
who through faith and patience inherit what has been promised.*

HEBREWS 6:12 NIV

O Lord, each of us is blessed to be part of Your divine plan, one of many who inherit the promises. Thank You for those who have gone before, paving the way, showing us how to live by faith. We treasure Your Word and the people we meet therein. They're like us—having questions and difficulties. Like them, we learn to walk by faith even as we endeavor to teach others.

Receiving the Reward

And whatever you do, do it heartily, as to the Lord and not to men,
knowing that from the Lord you will receive the reward of the inheritance;
for you serve the Lord Christ.
COLOSSIANS 3:23–24 NKJV

*L*ord Jesus, we are privileged to serve You. When nobody appreciates our efforts, when students are uncooperative, when we are misunderstood—in all these things, we remind ourselves that our service is for You, not for people. Thank You for living this in Your life, so we can follow You, serving wholeheartedly, knowing our reward is in You.

Carrying Sheaves

He who goes out weeping, carrying seed to sow,
will return with songs of joy, carrying sheaves with him.
PSALM 126:6 NIV

*F*ather, thank You that, as teachers, we can sow Your eternal seed, confident that even while we are weeping, there will be a harvest in Your time. We are blessed to carry this seed, blessed to care enough to weep over those with whom we share it, blessed to sing songs of joy as we return, bearing sheaves from the harvest. Surely this is worth spending our lives on—an eternal investment.

Our Treasure

"Store up for yourselves treasures in heaven, where moth and
rust do not destroy, and where thieves do not break in and steal.
For where your treasure is, there your heart will be also."
MATTHEW 6:20–21 NIV

Lord Jesus, how we need to reorder our priorities so that we are giving ourselves to what matters in Your sight. It's so easy to focus on the things around us—our homes and our classes, even our careers, and forget what it's all about. Keep us from accumulating stuff. May we invest our time and our energy in eternal treasure.

The Crown of Glory

And when the Chief Shepherd appears,
you will receive the crown of glory that will never fade away.
1 PETER 5:4 NIV

*L*ord Jesus, You are the pattern we can follow today as we lead our "sheep" to pasture. We help them find food, we try to protect them, we find them and bring them home when they are lost. What a privilege to make such an investment, which brings an eternal reward. The crown we win is unlike the trophies and medals that honor our earthly achievements. Its glory is unfading.

In His Steps

For you have been called for this purpose, since Christ also suffered for
you, leaving you an example for you to follow in His steps.
1 PETER 2:21 NASB

*L*ord Jesus, forgive me for wanting to take the easy road, forgetting the road You traveled led to a cross. Yet it didn't end there but continued from the tomb to a glorious resurrection. Help me remember Your victory when I'm tempted to focus on the suffering. Change my heart to be like Yours—submissive and obedient to the Father's plan.

Children, a Gift and a Reward

Behold, children are a gift of the LORD,
the fruit of the womb is a reward.
PSALM 127:3 NASB

*F*ather, what a blessed position we are in, to work with so many of Your gifts, the children in our classrooms. Each one is precious in Your sight. Help us to remember that when they're misbehaving or causing trouble. May we never lose sight of each child's value in Your eyes. Speak this message to them through us so they will know how much they are loved.

Conclusion

As I read books and magazine articles and talked to teachers in preparation for writing this book, I have been encouraged to see in how many ways teachers are impacting the lives of students out of the strong sense of commitment that drives them to reach out and make a difference. I see, as never before, how many members of the Body of Christ are on the front lines in our schools, fighting to bring Jesus to the next generation.

Often they work in difficult situations, making do in less-than-adequate circumstances. But educators are a tough breed! They know what their students need intellectually, emotionally, and spiritually. And they seize every opportunity to dispense information, love, and security, along with faith to help meet the many needs that exist.

Dawn, a forty-year teaching veteran, said she believes teachers pray more than those in other professions because "as a group we feel, or at least hope, that we make an impact on the lives of our students." Many others echoed her sentiment. I discovered that teachers make tremendous sacrifices because of their commitment to the profession. My own director drives over three hundred miles each week to teach two classes, out of her love for her job and her students.

I have observed several good habits that I hope to

include in my own prayer life. Some teachers pray in the room each morning before students arrive. Some bow beside specific desks interceding for individual students and needs. And they see the Lord answer faithfully. Judy, a tutor, put it best: "The Lord's care becomes my care." And His care touches people, making an eternal difference.

Like John, I feel no book could hold all there is to tell about these educators. I learned of teachers being changed as they allowed God to soften their hearts toward difficult students. And I learned of students' lives being changed as teachers faithfully shared new life with them in Christ. All across the country, even beyond our borders, lives are being impacted by teachers like you and me. In large ways and small ways, we are making a difference.

I have learned that teachers are also learners. We never graduate from the school of life. The world is our classroom, and often our students are our best instructors. At the end of his book *Teach Like Your Hair's on Fire*, Rafe Esquith includes an essay by a former student describing how her life was changed through his class. He prefaces the student's words with his own feeling that sometimes it is difficult to find a reason to believe we can make a difference. Yet her words helped him realize, as each of us knows, it's all worth it. God often gives us such glimpses to encourage us and keep us going, especially when we are having a hard time and we are tempted to give up.

As I read books on prayer, I was humbled by the depth and vision of writers from a variety of backgrounds over hundreds of years. From prison cells and pain as well as strength and victory, they poured out their love for the Lord with the lessons they have learned from hours and years of communion with Him.

Watchman Nee shared the following illustration in his book *Let Us Pray*:

> *Prayer is the rail for God's work. Indeed, prayer is to God's will as rails are to a train. The locomotive is full of power: It is capable of running a thousand miles a day. But if there are no rails, it cannot move forward a single inch. If it dares to move without them, it will soon sink into the earth. It may be able to travel over great distances, yet it cannot go to any place where no rails have been laid.*

May we cooperate with the Lord in laying rails through prayer. Let us put down the tracks with which He can accomplish His will through us.

Prayer is an exciting journey in which we share an intimate and loving relationship with our heavenly Father. Through this book, I have come a ways along the path, but I realize I have much further to go. I am awed by God's constant availability and His eagerness to meet me and travel with me on my journey of faith. I believe, now more than ever, the best is yet to be.

Other Power Prayers Titles

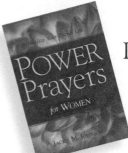

Power Prayers for Women
by Jackie M. Johnson

ISBN 978-1-59789-670-2

Power Prayers for Men
by John Hudson Tiner

ISBN 978-1-59789-858-4

Power Prayers for Mothers
by Rachel Quillin

ISBN 978-1-59789-998-7

Power Prayers to
Start Your Day
by Donna K. Maltese

ISBN 978-1-59789-859-1

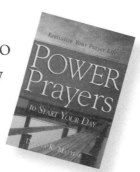